Catechesis in a Multimedia World

Editorial Board
Paulist Catechetical Guide Series

Editor
Jean Marie Hiesberger

Consultants
Sr. Kate Dooley, OP
Sr. Edith Prendergast
Michael Horan
Maruja Sedano
Gloria Durka

Catechesis in a Multimedia World

CONNECTING TO TODAY'S STUDENTS

Mary Byrne Hoffmann

Paulist Press
New York/Mahwah, NJ

The Scripture quotations contained herein are from the *New Revised Standard Version: Catholic Edition* Copyright © 1989 and 1993, by the Division of Christian Education of the National Council of the Churches of Christ in the United States of America. Used by permission. All rights reserved.

Grateful acknowledgment is made to the Center for Media Literacy/www.medialit.org for permission to use the Empowerment Spiral on page 42 and the table on page 67. Both are taken from their guide *Literacy for the 21st Century: An Overview & Orientation Guide to Media Literacy Education.*

Copyright © 2011 by Mary Byrne Hoffmann

All rights reserved. No part of this book may be reproduced or transmitted in any form or by any means, electronic or mechanical, including photocopying, recording, or by any information storage and retrieval system without permission in writing from the Publisher.

Library of Congress Cataloging-in-Publication Data

Hoffmann, Mary Byrne.
  Catechesis in a multimedia world : connecting to today's students / by Mary Byrne Hoffmann.
    p. cm.
  ISBN 978-0-8091-4708-3 (alk. paper)
  1. Catechetics--Catholic Church. 2. Christian education of teenagers. 3. Mass media--Religious aspects--Catholic Church--Study and teaching. 4. Catholic Church--Education. I. Title.
  BX1968.H56 2011
  268'.820285--dc22

2010040488

Published by Paulist Press
997 Macarthur Boulevard
Mahwah, New Jersey 07430

www.paulistpress.com

Printed and bound in the United States of America

Contents

Part One: The Media Pilgrimage
3

1. Welcome to a New World
5

2. The Media Pilgrimage
10

3. The Story
15

4. The Journey
23

5. The Known World of the Gospel
32

6. The Unknown World of Media
38

7. The Sacred Encounter
46

8. Transformation: A View from the Bridge
52

Part Two: Media Ministry
57

9. A Guide to Part Two
59

10. Media Ministry
61

11. Core Concept #1: The Audience Negotiates Meaning
73

12. Core Concept #2: All Media Construct Reality
89

13. Core Concept #3: Media Messages Use a Creative Language with Its Own Rules
99

14. Core Concept #4: Media Are Businesses Organized for Profit and Power
107

15. Core Concept #5: Media Shape Values
117

Notes
123

True story. A little girl, eight years old, goes to visit her grandmother, who is sick. She brings along her cell phone and iPod because she always brings along her cell phone and iPod. When she enters Grandma's bedroom, her attention is instantly drawn to a pair of rosary beads hanging on the bed.

"Grandma, what are those?" the little girl asks with great curiosity.

"Oh, my dear," says Grandma. "They are my rosary beads."

The little girl is puzzled. "What do you do with rosary beads?"

Grandma says, "Well, I use them to pray and to talk to God."

The girl's eyes widen with glee. "Oh! Grandma, where do you plug them in?"

Part One:
The Media Pilgrimage

1
Welcome to a New World

Every September, I walk to the podium in the front of the classroom and face the same audience. Sitting in undersized desks, the half-in, half-out bodies of 150 senior high school students mimic a similar level of ambivalent mental engagement. Newly and unhappily disconnected from their constant companions—the beloved iPod, the faithful cell phone, and the wonderful world of 24/7 Web surfing—they have been shorn of all familiar landmarks by the rules and regulations of school. I look at them, stuffed, suffocating, and adrift in mourning. How can I possibly compete with their world of constant stimulation and instant gratification? As if they sense my predicament, their bold stares lob back the ultimatum of the expecting-to-be-utterly-bored: Make my day.

Face-to-face after a long summer, I am once again reminded of how different the worlds of student and teacher are. The generation gap that separates us is child's play compared to the culture gap that estranges us. It takes a deep breath and another look at all those expectant faces to remember the obvious: I am on a mission to another universe.

That universe, called the "media culture,"[1] is the destination of this book. Undoubtedly, you have come across some of its inhabitants. Talking out loud to invisible parties, oblivious to the world around them, in a state of perpetual distraction, they send and receive thousands of transmissions from remote locations via instruments held in their hands or plugged into their ears. Each of those transmissions carries messages that tell stories, transmit values, define lifestyles, and shape reality. Most of these messages—whether positive or negative, hidden or overt—are consumed and created by our children and youth without any context or filter provided by a teacher, preacher, or parent. Ironically, the technology that delivers this vast universe of unlimited, interactive, interconnected information has also shrunk the interrelational world of its customers to a community of one. Relationship takes place in the isolated cubicle of remote communication via Facebook, instant messaging, and text messaging. Even more alarming is that information—not learning—is processed without the benefit of critical thinking and viewing skills. What does this bode for catechesis in a culture where value messages are unfiltered by the moral lens of biblical tradition and spiritual wisdom so integral to faith formation?

Perhaps, this is the question that propelled you to read this book because it speaks to a growing inability to connect with your "connected" students. Dislocation is the source of their disengagement and your frustration. The youth today roam a universe dominated by images (media culture); most teachers are still grounded on a planet dominated by words (print culture). This cultural divide rears its ugly head in the middle of a failed lesson plan. We are teaching the critical thinking skills needed to function in the print culture, while our students are floundering in a digital deluge of images without the critical viewing skills to navigate the media culture. Both of us are falling into the abyss of noncommunication and disconnection.

The solution is clear. As teachers, we have to bridge the chasm to create a learning environment that critiques, interprets, and integrates a culture that is rapidly changing the way that knowledge and information is delivered, received, processed, and distributed. As catechists, who are charged with the care of souls, we need to venture into this new universe on a threefold mission:

1. To discover for ourselves the many possibilities that the media culture offers catechesis;
2. To develop the critical skills and moral compass necessary for the responsible and effective use of visual media (film, television programs) and digital resources (blogs, wiks, Facebook, Google Docs) in our teaching methods; and
3. To teach those skills to our students, so they can understand how multimedia messages shape their sense of meaning and ultimately form their faith.

This is your guidebook to the universe of the media culture.

STRUCTURE OF THE BOOK
Spiritual Formation

This book is divided into two sections. *Part One: The Media Pilgrimage* is a journey into the media culture. It is designed to immerse the catechist into a personal encounter with a wide range of mass media. In many ways, the media pilgrimage is like going on a retreat. The interactive readings and activities encourage you to put aside time to experience and reflect upon media content and technology from television programs to podcasts to blogs to Facebook. The suggested pace of this media retreat is deliberate and contemplative. Your most important task is to cultivate the spiritual discipline of awareness by observing your thoughts and feelings while watching a movie or surfing the Net. When you become aware of media's influence, you realize its power to shape our values. When you understand that power in the context of gospel values, you are better able to filter media messages and lead your students on the same journey.

Faith Formation

It has been said that a person goes on retreat in order to advance further into the world. That is exactly the dynamics of how spiritual transformation affects faith formation. You bring the transformative experience and insights of your pilgrimage into the classroom to more effectively relate media to the Gospel.

Part Two: Media Ministry is a workshop that provides you with the tools to go forth and preach the good news in a multimedia environment and to better minister to the needs of your students. Specifically, you will be introduced to media literacy. Media literacy is the ability to read, evaluate, analyze, and create all forms of visual and digital media. Based on five core concepts that promote critical thinking and viewing skills, media literacy will give you a working framework for examining how media messages reflect and evolve the gospel messages.

GOD IN OUR MIDST

In his book *The Holy Longing*, Ronald Rolheiser makes an important distinction regarding the meaning of the name "Jesus the Christ," which is how I will refer to Jesus throughout the book. Rolheiser is quick to point out that "Christ" is not the surname of a man who lived and died over two thousand years ago. Rather, Christ is the meaning of who Jesus is in the present moment and for all time to come: he is the incarnated God who dwells among us in Eucharist and who is mediated through community to the world. Jesus the Christ is God in our midst.

Karl Rahner, the renowned twentieth-century theologian, spoke about Jesus the Christ as God's self-communication. This magnificent gesture infers an ongoing dialogue in which God persists in being revealed in this world, in these times, through human relationship and communication. Somewhere in all those media messages that we consume on a daily basis through the iPod, the cell phone, Facebook, video games, and BlackBerries, there is the potential to hear the voice and see the face of God in those who are made in the image of God. At the threshold of the third millennium, as we live through one of the most important cultural and spiritual transformations in history, we cannot afford to miss the enduring miracle of the presence of God in our world as it is, in our midst as we are.

2
The Media Pilgrimage

> The convergence of media and technology in a global culture is changing the way we learn about the world and challenging the very foundation of education. No longer is it enough to be able to read the printed word; children, youth, and adults, too, need the ability to both critically interpret the powerful images of a multimedia culture and express themselves in multiple media forms.
>
> —*Sr. Liz Thoman, Founder, Center for Media Literacy*

You are about to embark on a media pilgrimage. All pilgrims throughout time and religious traditions leave what is familiar for a road less traveled in order to find God. You, the media pilgrim, are no different. Your quest is to explore the relatively unknown landscape of spiritual transformation and faith formation in a media age. At the heart of this quest are questions that challenge the relevancy of catechesis. Is media Gospel? Is Gospel media? Are media and Gospel in competition for the hearts and souls of the twenty-first-century audience? Is there a conflict between the values formation of mass media and the spiritual formation of the Gospel? Is it possible to find God in the media? How does the catechist make the Gospel relevant to the "digital" generations? Can media be an effective tool for catechesis? What is the role of the catechist in the media culture?

The Path of Gospel and Media

These questions will serve as your compass on the pilgrimage pointing you always in the direction of your destination: a greater understanding of the relationship between Gospel and media. Along the way, you will be guided by the assurance that the Gospel is alive and dynamic throughout time. That, in fact, as Gospel transforms culture, culture gives new meaning to the Gospel. This is the meaning of the incarnation. Jesus took on flesh, became human, lived in this world, and used this world to reveal the realm of God. In the same way that Jesus embodies both humanity and divinity, the Gospel continues to connect the story of Jesus the Christ with the evolving story of humankind.

There is no separating Gospel from culture. As the twentieth-century mystic Evelyn Underhill said so well, "We are agents of the Creative Spirit in this world." Our role as catechists is not just to preach the Gospel but to find the Gospel wherever we are. The Gospel is never taught in a vacuum but in the context of human beings living out their lives in this world on a daily basis. In today's technological, multisensory environment of rapid information and omnipresent images, discipleship means taking to the seven-hundred-channel universe to first explore and then preach the presence of God in the media culture.

This underlying partnership of culture and spirit is integral to catechesis. At the core of religious education is the transmission of gospel values. The reality is that today's students are more likely to consume values information from the pervasive messages of the media culture than scripture. Spiritual transformation partners with faith formation to teach and nurture the whole person. In order to do this successfully, we must provide students with the critical viewing tools to navigate popular culture as informed persons of faith. This means that we filter the value messages of media through the lens of the Gospel.

Media Pilgrimage

The journey to this new way of seeing faith and culture begins in Chapter 3 with a look at how storytelling throughout time reflects and evolves our search for God. Chapter 4 introduces you to the power of images in gospel and media stories. In Chapter 5, you will explore how Jesus used the particular images in parables to suggest another reality—the realm of God. The next step in any pilgrimage is leaving the comfort zone of what is known to be surprised by God in the obstacles and the opportunities of the unknown. In the media pilgrimage, this means venturing into the media landscape to find the holy. Chapter 6 plunges you into the world of mass media images that construct today's reality—the realm of culture.

The realm of God and the realm of culture meet in Chapter 7 where you stand on a bridge connecting the two realities. This is the place of divine encounter where hopefully you begin to see Gospel and media in a different light. Without giving away the end of the story, Chapters 7 and 8 present you with both the gifts and responsibilities of undertaking the media pilgrimage. At the end of Chapters 3 through 8, there will be television and movie suggestions, internet activities, and reflection exercises for you to process what you are learning along the way.

True to the dynamics of pilgrimage, as you travel this path, you will encounter angels and demons. It is important to welcome them both. You will be sometimes dismayed and even discouraged by the moral and spiritual vacuity of media fare playing on primetime television and in your local theaters. You will also be amazed and encouraged by media's many exquisitely crafted messages of faith, hope, and love. As Jesus often prodded his disciples, "Stay awake!" Experience everything along the way. Hold out for the surprises!

Media Ministry

The second part of the book is the application phase. After having been introduced and hopefully converted to the possibilities of media to transmit the Gospel, Part Two sends you forth as media ministers to preach the good news in the media culture. In Chapters 9 through 15, you will learn the practical tools and skills for integrating media into your catechetical programs. This section focuses on Five Concepts of Media Literacy and also includes a Tool Box section at the end of each chapter with media recommendations, curriculum suggestions, and related activities for grades 1 through 12.

ON YOUR WAY

All pilgrims are accompanied by guides. The media pilgrimage can be undertaken alone or in a group of catechists as an ongoing in-service retreat/workshop. If you choose to go alone, be sure to get some advice along the way from media experts in your midst. Your children or your students are a good choice. The media is their first language. They can help you navigate the weekly TV guide, download music and podcasts, and maybe set up your own Facebook page! They will also provide valuable insights into their viewing habits. If you are a parent, watch television with your children. This is how you begin to model the practice of filtering the message.

It's always best to travel lightly, especially when you are expecting the Spirit. However, I do suggest that you take along the following items on your media pilgrimage: a journal or notebook, the Bible, the weekly TV guide, the cultural and entertainment section of your local newspaper (in print or online), an open mind, and a willing disposition. Make sure you always know where the remote is!

A GUIDING THOUGHT

Every journey provides a clue to send the traveler off in the right direction. So, here is a guiding thought for your trip through the media universe: Jesus used parable—the medium of his time—to tell the story of the human-divine relationship. Two thousand years later, with limitless media possibilities, how will you continue to tell that same story?

3
The Story

When the founder of Hasidic Judaism, the great Rabbi Israel Shem Tov, saw misfortune threatening the Jews, it was his custom to go into a certain part of the forest to meditate. There he would light a fire, say a special prayer, and the miracle would be accomplished, and the misfortune averted.

Later, when his disciple, the celebrated Maggid of Mezritch, had occasion for the same reason to intercede with heaven, he would go to the same place in the forest and say, "Master of the Universe, listen! I do not know how to light the fire, but I am still able to say the prayer." Again, the miracle would be accomplished.

Still later, Rabbi Moshe-leib of Sasov, in order to save his people once more, would go into the forest and say, "I do not know how to light the fire. I do not know the prayer, but I know the place, and this must be sufficient." It was sufficient, and the miracle was accomplished.

Then it fell to Rabbi Israel of Rizhin to overcome misfortune. Sitting in his armchair with his head in his hands, he spoke to God, "I am unable to light the fire, and I do not know the prayer, and I cannot even find the place in the forest. All I can do is to tell the story, and this must be sufficient."

And it was sufficient. For God made humankind because God loves stories.[1]

This is a book about stories. The way we tell them. Why we tell them. Who tells them. And, probably most important, what stories say about human beings and our relationship to God.

Every story, no matter where or when it is told, asks and answers a question about the mystery of being human. Ultimately, all meaningful inquiries about life are about being in or out of right relationship to ourselves and to one another. And in most religions those questions, which are the curiosities of the soul, lead right to our relationship with the Holy Mystery, who is God. Stories bring to consciousness the yearning at the heart of the human-divine relationship: We are creatures in search of our Creator. "The desire for God is written in the human heart."[2]

This timeless longing for God seems to be hardwired into the human soul. It is a certainty. It is a question. It is a curiosity. Embrace God, reject God, ignore God; this is the stuff of all our stories as we try to explain the good, the bad, and the mystery of the human drama. Every story is a hand reaching across the universe to connect with something greater than ourselves.

Once upon a Time

Nowhere is this pursuit of God more dramatic than in sacred scripture. The epic stories of many religious traditions tell spellbinding tales of the heights to which we ascend and the depths to which we fall, depending on our connection or disconnection to God. Stories of creation and destruction, good and evil, suffering and redemption, death and life thread through time and across cultures attesting to the perils of the fragile human condition graced by love or disgraced by fear. Whether we gathered around tribal fires, listened to sermons on mountaintops, gleaned the life of Jesus from stained glass windows, read Paul's passion in a printed Bible or sit in darkened theaters riveted to the multisensory storytelling of cinema, we tell stories of hope and despair for the same reasons: We are roaming the nooks and crannies of mystery in search of answers. What we pursue is the riddle of our origin, our purpose, our destiny, and the Source of this tremendous human longing for communion that nothing on earth can ever seem to satisfy. The grand themes of our narratives have not altered throughout time.

What has changed is the way that we tell stories. As the tools of storytelling evolved from oral communication to the written word to the printed word to electronic mass media, our perception of reality was transformed on every level. How we tell our stories seems to have a direct correlation to our changing sense of self, others, and God. The advanced technology of storytelling mirrors the evolution of the human soul. With every shift in the means of our communication, there has been a parallel movement in the development of spirituality and culture.

The Media Timeline

The history of story is characterized by three distinct eras, each one defined by different tools—technology—for storytelling: the Oral Age (spoken word), the Print Age (written and printed word), and the Media Age (visual and digital communication). Although each era spans a certain period of time, this does not mean that one mode of storytelling extinguished and replaced another. Indeed, oral storytelling is experiencing a popular resurgence today. Similarly, there are many people today who believe that the age of the printed word is dimming in the neon lights of the age of media. But, this does not mean the end of best-sellers and bedtime stories. The dates simply indicate how the emerging dominant technology or medium of expression within a given time frame shaped faith and culture.

The Age of the Spoken Word: 90,000–3100 BC

In the earliest stages of human history, stories were passed on through the spoken word. The art of storytelling was a sacred mantle worn by tribal elders who channeled the spiritual world and cloaked life with meaning. These revered men and women explained the mysteries of daily life—birth, death, love, fear, suffering, joy—in myths that imagined another time and place where wounds were healed, lessons were learned, justice was served.

What was unique to the primitive consciousness was the absolute belief that the material and the spiritual worlds were one reality. Mystified by the puzzle of the created universe, the Homo sapiens of twenty thousand years ago intuited the presence of the Divine who was not only everywhere but "everywhen"[3] making of everything a sacrament.

The earliest spoken stories were an emotional testament to the sense of the unknown that pervaded consciousness of the ancients. The terror and beauty of the natural world inspired fear and awe. The randomness of life and death commanded humility and obedience. The prehistoric man and woman saw themselves as creatures at the mercy of gods and goddesses somewhere out there—in the sun, the moon, the wind, the rain, in life, and in death. This powerful pantheon of deities molded, guided, punished, and rewarded all manner of human behavior. In the Age of the Spoken Word, the Creator was the main protagonist of the human story.

The Age of the Written and Printed Word: 3100 BC–AD 1950

Around 3100 BC, the written word emerged in the Middle East. It did not immediately replace the spoken word, but over centuries, writing the story and then printing the story became the dominant means of telling the story. By the time Jesus the Christ was born two thousand years ago, the written word was becoming the preferred means of communication among the educated classes.

It is therefore interesting to note that as far as we know, Jesus—who was a noted rabbi, schooled in Jewish tradition and scripture—did not leave behind any writings. Instead, he was an itinerant preacher, a storyteller, a healer who went from town to town proclaiming the spoken word. It was only after Jesus' death and resurrection that his story was written down, first by Paul, beginning around 50 AD, and then successively by the evangelists: Mark, Matthew, Luke, and John in the latter half of the first century AD.

Literacy moved the Gospel beyond Jerusalem into Asia Minor. Eventually, the printing press moved the Gospel to the farthest regions of the world. *The Catechism* and the Catholic educational system were both astute and timely responses to the challenge of evangelization in the print age. In fact, there was no aspect of human existence that was not radically changed by the invention of the printing press, in 1456, when Gutenberg bound the first printed Bible.

In the print age, storytelling moved from the heart to the head. Reading and writing were learned communication skills. In the western hemisphere, tribal fires were extinguished to pave the town square where stories were passed on in schoolbooks and church Bibles. Printing, even more than writing, committed the story to words set in ink. There was a certainty and authority to the fixed word on the page that was not found in the more fluid spoken word. The wise elders of the oral age were replaced by the new storytellers of the print age—knowledgeable scholars, well-versed preachers, and eventually the scientists of logic, reason, and proof.

The Age of the Printed Word was the age of humankind. It was a time when we pushed the boundaries of the mind to create stories of a world evolving in our image. Our accomplishments in every field of human endeavor were astounding—organized religions, complex societies, classical literature, modern medicine, atomic weapons. There seemed to be nothing that we could not create or destroy. But an age that relies predominantly on the logic of the mind starves a soul that is nurtured by faith. Somewhere, in between the lines of theory and doctrine, in the glare of our intellect and reason, we lost sight of God.

The Age of Mass Media: 1900–Present

The media age is, of course, the subject of this book and is yours to discover in the remaining pages. In one of the activities below, you are asked to write down a few thoughts profiling the particular characteristics of the media age as you begin this journey. At the conclusion of this book, you will have another opportunity to comment on the media age, however, this time from the perspective of having undertaken the media pilgrimage.

Spiritual Exercises

These exercises will take you through time as you experience the same story in three different ways: spoken, read, and viewed. At the end of the exercise, please take some time to reflect on it in your journal. Suggestions are provided below.

1. The Story: The Nativity (Luke 1:26–56; 2:1–21)

As you listen, read, and view the same story through different media, observe how you are engaged by each rendering. Don't make any comparisons or judgments. Just note how your intellect, senses, imagination, and spirituality are engaged.

a. *Listen*: Begin by listening to the spoken story. Ask someone to read the scripture passage to you. After hearing

the story, spend some quiet time in the echo of the spoken word. Then take a moment to reflect in your journal about how you experienced the story.
b. *Read*: Read the same passage silently. Be silent for a few moments, and then, note any responses to the reading of the story in your journal.
c. *View*: Watch the movie, *The Nativity Story* (Rated PG, 2006). Take a walk after the movie or just sit quietly and notice how the movie affects you—mind, body, and soul. Put your feelings to words in your journal.

2. Media Age Reflection

Based on what you know about the media culture right now—at the start of your pilgrimage—how would you describe the media age? You might want to address technology, audience, the impact of media on catechesis, how mass media changes the human-divine relationship, who is at the center of the story in the media age. At the end of this book, you will have an opportunity to revise your initial response.

4
The Journey

The feeling remains that God is on the journey, too.
—*St. Teresa of Avila*

THE MEDIA LANDSCAPE

For the pilgrim searching for God in the media culture, here's the good news: The life and times of Jesus the Christ that have captivated audiences for more than two thousand years continue to draw crowds today. The bad news is that the life and times of today's number one hot celebrity trending on Twitter may be stealing the show. Is the Gospel a lone voice in the wilderness of tabloid morality? Or is something else happening here? Something inviting us beyond the gossipy sound bites and the provocative images to reconcile the world of media with the realm of the Spirit?

In the face of the facts, reconciliation may seem ambitious. On an ordinary night in American households, the television fare runs the gamut from desperate housewives, to mad men, to cutthroat survivors. Switch over to cable and go from bad to worse: 24/7 newscasts peppered with lurid headlines, grown-ups ranting and raving with divisive commentary, X-rated stand-up comedy—and that's just a few out of the over seven hundred channels. Glued to their TV screens, mostly alone in their rooms, millions of youngsters prefer the vicarious thrill and sensation of the multimedia experience to the seemingly more passive and monolithic experience of listening to the Gospel in a church pew.

The Media Gods

Electronic mass media permeates every facet of our lives. That, in fact, is the nature of mass media. Ironically, it is also the role of religion. In the media landscape of the twenty-first century, the God who is "everywhere" seems to have been preempted by the gods of mass media—Information, Consumerism, Gratification, Sensation—who are everywhere, all the time, no matter what. You can turn off the TV, but you cannot turn off the culture. It is there waiting for you wherever you are waiting—in doctors' offices, at gas station pumps, at bus stops, in airports. The list goes on. The television, the Internet, the cell phone never go off.

Commercials, like all visual media, create a multisensory environment for the viewer. I call this an "emotional field" because it immediately charges the viewer with an avalanche of sensations triggered by images, sound, music, and lighting.

Several years ago, in the middle of the World Series, there was a very creative and effective promotional commercial for ESPN (24/7 sports network) playing on, of course, ESPN. The commercial opens with a simple but stark image: "4:32 a.m." in white lettering against a black screen. Right away, the commercial evokes the emotional field of high anxiety in the middle of a sleepless night. A deep patriarchal voice rattles off a series of dark night questions along the line of "Why am I here? Am I loved? Is there a God?" And then to the tune of "Take Me out to the Ball Game" subtly shifting into Gregorian chant (a very unobtrusive but successful emotional prompt), the final question is posed: Did the Yankees beat the Twins? Message: ESPN answers the really important questions 24/7 unlike those annoying little soul-searching questions that keep you awake while God is sleeping on the job. The God who is everywhere has been usurped by the cable network that is everywhere. What is so remarkable about this commercial is that it uses primal spiritual yearnings and traditional religious music to sell a product. In other words, it co-opts religious values to seduce the audience without the audience even knowing that they have been seduced. That's great advertising but lousy theology!

The Challenge for Catechists

ESPN is not alone in its use of religious symbolism and sentiment to lure potential viewers (consumers). Such tactics are regularly employed by advertisers to attract a customer base. And so, the questions beg: Whose values are they anyway? Are we losing our audience? The easy response is to blame the media. The more difficult solution is to counter by telling our stories in the language of our time just as Jesus employed the language of his times. The charismatic preacher who spoke to the people two thousand years ago in parables used the storytelling medium of Palestinian culture. What would Jesus do today? Undoubtedly, he would speak to us in today's language of the multimedia culture. Undoubtedly, he is. The better question is: Are we listening?

THE MISSION

Intrinsic to every pilgrimage is the spiritual art of listening. As we journey, we open ourselves to hear the voice of God's discernment directing us to our purpose. Your mission as catechists in the media age is fourfold:

1. To become critically aware of the role of mass media in values formation through the contemplative disciplines of listening to and observing media with an open mind and spirit;
2. To identify gospel values in media messages;
3. To build a bridge linking Gospel and media in your catechetical approach to faith formation so that your students can walk across it into the world as informed persons of faith; and
4. To become storytellers in the twenty-first century by speaking the language of our times, which means using the media to continue to tell the ongoing story of the human-divine relationship.

THE WAY

The media pilgrimage begins, as do all journeys, in the known world with who you are and where you are. In this case, it is as a catechist teaching in the twenty-first century that you set out to explore the reach of the Gospel into today's popular culture.

According to the Catholic Church, the Gospel is sacred scripture that tells the story of the life and teaching of Jesus the Christ. That's the official definition according to the *Catechism*. But, we don't live by definitions alone. We also live by understandings that come from being alive, from finding our way through the human experience to a relationship with God. Jesus himself embodies and models this path in his humanity. When Thomas asks Jesus, "How can we know the way?" Jesus replies, "I am the way, and the truth, and the life" (John 14:5–6). The Gospel is a way of life that speaks to a way of being in the world. It is not a set of directions. It is a map. Your work as catechists is to find the map, follow the path, and serve as guides along the way to the Way.

The Map

The way of life prescribed by Jesus was like manna in the desert for the "great crowds that followed him." In a poignant illustration of the ragtag humanity that sought solace from Jesus, Matthew describes the multitudes as "the sick, those afflicted with various diseases and pains, demoniacs, epileptics, and paralytics" (Matt 4:24). We know from other Gospels that "the thousands of the multitudes" (Luke 12:1) who flocked to see, hear, and touch Jesus during most of his ministry also included the sinner, the poor, the stranger, the women—all cast aside by society.

Mesmerized by his message of inclusivity, the outcasts were welcomed back into their humanity through the compassionate humanity of Jesus the Christ. He forgave their sins, healed their wounds, called them to be disciples, sat with them, dined with them, and laughed with them. But most importantly, he dignified the marginalized by making them the heroes and heroines of his stories—the woman at the well, the tax collector, the publican, the possessed, the paralytic. Jesus restored their birthright as images of God by imaging them in stories. In seeing them in the light of his divine heart, he opened their hearts to another way of seeing themselves and God.

Stories are the language of the heart. Jesus told stories because he knew that they are doorways out of the small space of human misery into the much larger space of human possibility. Stories open up the "I" to see the "we" and as such are the connective tissue of relationships. By opening the heart, they bring us to another way of understanding ourselves, one another, and God. For the people who walked with Jesus two thousand years ago, stories were the healing balms rejoining the throngs who were disconnected from society into a community of the Spirit. For those early followers, as well as those who follow Jesus in the twenty-first century, the stories of the New Testament are the maps pointing us in the direction of the realm of God.

The Clues

Recently, I asked about thirty students, all juniors in high school, to describe Jesus. Without exception, the students responded with images—Jesus in the manger, Jesus walking on water, Jesus calming the storm, Jesus on the cross, Jesus risen from the tomb. Asked when they formed these images, the students recalled the early years of elementary school when they learned about their faith through Bible stories. Over the years, their textbook knowledge of Jesus in high school did not change this earlier visual experience of Jesus. Despite all the information about church teachings related to Jesus the Christ, their formative and enduring experience of Jesus resided not in the facts but in the images.

If stories are the maps, then images are the clues. If stories are the language of the heart, images are the language of the soul. Images speak to and open up the heart that desires God. In the words of Pedro Arrupe, SJ, "Nothing is more practical than finding God, that is, than falling in love in a quite absolute, final way." A person's first encounter with Jesus through the images of story is a lot like falling in love.

When two people first meet in that timeless place of intrigue and infatuation, their imagination is seized by a longing to move beyond themselves and connect with another human being. They look across the table at one another and begin to tell stories about their favorite places, their best friends, their funniest moments, about growing up, and falling down and getting back up again. As they tell stories, images form of this new person and invite an experience of the other that transcends all precaution and hesitation. The stranger is clothed with garments of desire.

Likewise, as we listen to the stories that Jesus tells his followers, the images open our hearts to the experience of Jesus as a teacher, preacher, healer, and redeemer. We are radically changed at our core. We fall in love with Jesus not in a pious manner but out of a sense of familiarity that inspires awe and reverence. We are touched when he touches upon the mutuality of our shared humanity. This is called *metanoia*—a change of heart. It is the transforming spirit of the Gospels that allows us to see Jesus as the Divine Light who images the way to the Way.

This understanding of the power of gospel images is critical to faith formation in our time. Students today live in an image world of multisensory experience not dogma. Whereas most of us grew up in a world where love was conditioned by knowledge, in today's culture knowledge is inspired by love. Pierre Babin, in his book *The New Era in Religious Communication*, states this simply: "It is not theology or the catechism, but an open heart that makes Jesus lovable."[1] Or as Jesus says in Luke 12:35, "Where your treasure is, there your heart will also be."

The clues that lead us to the bridge connecting the two worlds of Gospel and media are found in the images of the gospel stories. The next step in the journey is to decipher and follow the clues.

Spiritual Exercises

1. Whose Values Are They Anyway?

What is love? What does it mean to be "awake" to life? Check out how a Super Bowl commercial and a scripture passage respond to the same questions.

a. Watch the Diet Pepsi Max commercial on YouTube. To view the commercial, go to:
   http://www.youtube.com/watch?v=UVYzxxgKXTY.
b. Now using the online Bible study site, Bible Study Tools, read the selected New Testament passages that address what it means to be "awake."

1. Go to www.biblestudytools.com.
2. Enter "awake" in the search field.
3. Choose "New Testament" in the "filter results" drop-down menu.
4. Click on the "Search" button. This will bring up all references to "awake" in the New Testament.

c. Compare the two meanings of *awake*.
d. Think about how the concept of love is used in this commercial. How would you use this commercial in class to discuss the gospel meaning of love?

2. In the Image of God

Apply your observations in exercise 1 to a more extensive comparison of media and gospel value messages.

Plan to spend at least thirty minutes to an hour watching commercials. You can sit in front of the television, or you can go check out your favorite commercials on YouTube (www.youtube.com). Look for commercials that use religious concepts (love, hope, compassion, forgiveness, faith, doubt, seeking) to sell a product. Take notes on what you watch and where you go on YouTube. You might be able to use your sightings in the classroom.

5
The Known World of the Gospel

> Then God said, "Let us make humankind in our image, according to our likeness".... So God created humankind in his image, in the image of God he created them; male and female he created them.
>
> —*Genesis 1:26–27*

The mystery at the heart of the Christian journey begins in Genesis 1 with the story of creation. Speaking in images—the language of the soul inspired by the Spirit—the authors paint a stunning picture of a majestic universe called into being. Perhaps right now, when you read this excerpt from Genesis, you recalled your earliest experience of hearing that story. Perhaps your imagination once again leaped to envision, "Let there be light"; "Let there be a dome in the midst of the waters"; "Let birds fly above the earth." Who could have imagined such a world? That is the point of the story. The universe was created from Divine Imagination.

From the well of Divine Imagination, humankind was created in God's own image—male and female—creatures who would spend their days on earth imaging and imagining their Creator. Imagination, imaging, image is the language that we share with our Creator. Soul of the Universe to soul of humankind, we imagine one another over and over again.

Out of this divine conversation, Jesus was born into the world. "In the beginning was the Word, and the Word was with God, and the Word was God. He was in the beginning with God" (John 1:1–2). John is referring to the spoken word that articulates image. In the person of Jesus the Christ, God communicates with us through a being who completely and perfectly embodies both divine and human natures. As a flesh and blood messenger from the Spirit world, Jesus spoke the common language that all human beings share in the depths of their souls with the Soul of the Universe. In his parables, teachings, discourses, and pronouncements, Jesus used images to convey another reality— the realm of God.

IMAGINE THERE'S A HEAVEN

For many of the people who followed Jesus, the difficulties of living had no doubt robbed them of the hope to imagine another way of life. In the midst of this desolate existence, there walked among them a man who told stories about the kingdom of God.

> Then he looked up at his disciples and said: "Blessed are you who are poor, for yours is the kingdom of God" (Luke 6:20).

The "kingdom of God" ("kingdom of heaven" in Matthew's Gospel) is mentioned over one hundred times in the New

Testament. Long awaited by the Jewish people, the kingdom is the core of Jesus' message. In Luke 4:43, a tireless Jesus besieged by a crowd reluctant to let him go, makes it very clear why he must move on: "I must proclaim the good news of the kingdom of God to the other cities also; for I was sent for this purpose."

Over the centuries, biblical scholars have written volumes about the meaning of the kingdom. They have wrangled with the political, ethical, and spiritual interpretations of the kingdom as it weaves its way through the prophetic tradition of the Old Testament into the salvific tradition of the New Testament. But, what is complicated by words is simplified in image. For, when Jesus spoke about the kingdom of God, he used the imagery of parables.

> "With what can we compare the kingdom of God, or what parable will we use for it? It is like a mustard seed, which, when sown upon the ground, is the smallest of all the seeds on earth; yet when it is sown it grows up and becomes the greatest of all shrubs, and puts forth large branches, so that the birds of the air can make nests in its shade." With many such parables he spoke the word to them, as they were able to hear it; he did not speak to them except in parables, but he explained everything in private to his disciples (Mark 4:30–32).

Jesus deliberately used parable storytelling to speak about the kingdom. The consummate communicator, Jesus knew well what Marshall McCluhan, the twentieth-century media guru, proclaimed in 1964: "The medium is the message." Jesus used the medium of his age—the images of the parable—to get across an ageless truth about the nature of the kingdom. Like the image of the mustard seed, "the smallest of all the seeds," that defies all manner of outcome and grows into the "greatest of shrubs and becomes a tree" (Matt 13:31–32), the kingdom is quite simply not what you expect.

PRIMETIME PARABLES

Media images are a lot like parable images. They, too, are unexpected experiences not predictable facts. They pick us up where words leave us off and take us into another dimension. A former New Testament professor of mine called parables "world switching." The same can be said of media images that also have the power to take us somewhere else.

Since the 1950s, when television became a standard appliance in American homes, everything in our way of life has been turned upside down and inside out. Just think of the way that television has depicted and changed family life, religion, education, politics, and culture. Over the years, several people in my media workshops have commented on how television and specifically the glitz and glamour serials like *Dallas* and *Dynasty* made them suddenly aware, in hindsight, of their own material poverty. Before tuning into the Ewings or the Carringtons, they had been pretty content with their modest but unparalleled lives. But the sensationalizing and normalizing of the *Dallas/Dynasty* lifestyles made it seem that anyone of lesser means was outside the culture. Getting "rich and famous" at any cost was portrayed as the only way to "get in" and get noticed.

Of course, there have been many ways that media have changed our lives for the better. Would we be so conscious of racial, ethnic, and religious diversity if we did not experience, sometimes in very unsettling ways, the plethora of human expression, behavior, and belief in the news, in documentaries, in the movies? Has the global consciousness of the Internet broadened our horizons and opened up our hearts and minds at the same time it has jettisoned us out of parochial world views? Like the parables, media are changing the way that stories are told to make way for a new story of who we are in relationship to God.

The next step in the media pilgrimage will immerse you in the culture of media images where you can see and hear for yourselves and "test the spirits to see whether they are from God" (1 John 4:1).

Spiritual Exercises

1. Media Exercise: The Parables

Read aloud the parables in Matthew 13. What would Jesus have emphasized when he was telling the stories? What part of the stories might have jolted the listeners out of their complacency and perhaps despair to hear a message of hope and encouragement? What do the parables say about the realm of God?

2. Activity: The Parable Collage

After reading the seven parables in Matthew's Gospel, select images from newspapers or magazines that tell a story similar to any or all of the parables. This is not a thinking exercise. The idea is for you to experience the parables through images. Don't censor your selections. As you create the parable collage, let your intuition and creativity be your guide. Allow yourself to be taken somewhere unexpected.

3. Journal Exercise

What happened when you left the realm of words to look at parables through the lens of image? Did you move from an *understanding* of parable to an *experience* of parable? How is that experience different than reading or listening to an analysis of a parable?

6
The Unknown World of Media

> Toto, I have a feeling that we are not in Kansas anymore.
>
> —*Dorothy,* The Wizard of Oz

It is one of the most memorable scenes in the 1939 film *The Wizard of Oz*: Dorothy, a farm girl from Kansas, cringes in her bedroom clutching her dog, Toto, as she is hurled into the stratosphere by a fierce tornado. With a plop and pounce, she is abruptly tossed to the ground. For a brief suspended moment, Dorothy and everyone in the audience wonders where on earth she has landed. And then something happens that no one expects. Dorothy opens the unhinged door of her bedroom, walks out into the magical and strange Land of Oz, and, to her amazement, realizes that she is somewhere else.

When Dorothy opens the door, she was not the only one stunned. For, at that very moment, with that simple gesture, the audience in 1939 was transported from a black-and-white movie into a modern miracle of Technicolor as the Land of Oz lights up in primary colors. Later that same year, the first blockbuster movie, *Gone with the Wind*, was made entirely in Technicolor and swept the country off into another world of panoramic romance. We swooned with the power of big screen images that seemed to surround us, awakening all our senses. It was like being "there." It was not like being "here." It was, indeed, somewhere else.

THE SOMEWHERE ELSE

Welcome to the Media Age! From the time we get up in the morning and turn on the television or plug in the iPod, get in the car and turn on the radio, take in all the billboards that pave our road to work, we are practically drowning in a deluge of media images and messages. It's like thousands of munchkins talking at once. Overload!

This is the "unknown" part of the media pilgrimage not necessarily because you are in unfamiliar territory. Maybe you have learned to navigate the mediascape. Or maybe you can't quite figure it out and, like Dorothy, want to go back home to another time, another place that is more familiar. Wherever you are in your media comfort zone, you are probably overwhelmed. Too much information.[1] Too much entertainment. Too much violence. Too much sex. The media culture is unknown because most of us don't know how to navigate it— never mind guide our students through it.

MODERN PARABLE: THE MEDIA BASH

In Matthew 22:1–10, Jesus tells the story of a king who "gave a wedding banquet for his son." As you may recall, this king had a hard time getting people to come to his party. Time and again, he sent his slaves to "call those who had been invited" but to no avail. It seemed like everyone had better plans. Some of the guests, growing weary of the servants' pleas, crossed the line and "mistreated them and killed them." Enraged, the king then sent his troops who "destroyed those murderers and burned their cities." Not one to waste fattened oxen and slaughtered calves, the king then commands his servants to go into the streets and gather "all whom they found, both good and bad; so that the wedding hall was filled with guests."

In this parable, Jesus was making a statement about the kingdom of God. Let's use another kind of party but one with a set of very different guests to make a statement about the culture of mass media.

Instead of a wedding banquet, imagine what I call a "media bash"—a night at home just to kick back on the recliner and watch TV. Maybe, you are with family or friends. Maybe, you're on your own. Feet up, remote in hand, you are the king or queen of the castle. You turn on the TV to watch your favorite programs—your invited guests. But something unplanned happens. In addition to the invited guests, your party is crashed by a parade of uninvited guests—program reruns, endless commercials, talk show chatter, the no-real-news headlines, infomercials, infotainment. Garbed in the often confusing guise of information and/or entertainment, you let them in the door because there are no "attendants" like in Matthew 22:13 who will throw them out. For most of us, born and bred in a media culture, there is no bouncer at the front door to filter the 16,000 uninvited media messages that unconsciously bombard our consciousness every day.

The unknown territory of mass media is the unquestioned landscape. To paraphrase the Greek philosopher Plato, who wrote that "the unexamined life is not worth living," I would suggest that "the unexamined media are not worth watching." For the media pilgrim, to enter into the unknown is to enter into the questions of our time and culture. And that requires nothing less than a reflective and critical experience of our media in order to make choices—to decide what is "good and bad" so that your home and classroom can be filled with invited media messengers.

A Helpful Guide

In fact, media offer a range of experiences into the sacred. Like everything in our world, media are rich in sacramental moments that provide a profound experience of God. Films such as *Life Is Beautiful*, *The Spitfire Grill*, *Simon Birch*, *Norma Rae*, and *Mississippi Burning* revolve around characters (real and fictional) who lay down their lives for someone they love or something they believe in. They are modern-day Christ figures in contemporary stories of extraordinary courage and commitment.

The purpose of this phase of the media pilgrimage is for you to experience such moments. In order to do that, you'll have to sample a wide range of media. There are many wonderful programs and movies that will stun you with their truth, their wisdom, their hope—never mind visual beauty. You will be surprised by grace. On the other hand, you will also have to endure some very questionable programming. As is the case with any pilgrimage, the only way out is through the "dark forest" where the demons of primetime television may threaten your soul or, at the very least, your sense of decency. Dorothy takes the yellow brick road. You get to take a virtual tour through the universe of images. But be forewarned; you don't go alone.

In the Witches Forest, Dorothy found the three personal qualities that she needed in order to reach Oz—brains, compassion, and courage—in the persons of three unlikely friends—the scarecrow, the tin man, and the cowardly lion. The media pilgrim needs similar guidance in navigating the media landscape. The Empowerment Spiral, which was developed by the renowned Brazilian educator Paolo Freire, provides the media pilgrim with four equally worthy companions to guide you through the process of critical viewing: awareness, analysis, reflection, and action.

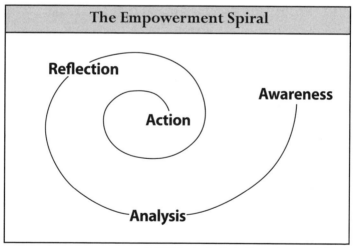

© 2008 Center for Media Literacy/www.medialit.org

The Empowerment Spiral is an ongoing and deepening exercise in media awareness. The first step asks you to simply be *aware* of what you are viewing. Instead of instinctively changing channels or websites to move on from what is uninteresting or offensive, the second step challenges you to stay with the program and *analyze* your response in terms of how particular media make you think or feel. The third step is to *reflect* on what influences your media choices: personal values and morals, political views, religious beliefs, parental concerns, world view, social justice. By becoming aware of what you watch or why you surf certain websites, you are no longer a passive audience shaped by media. Media choices are shaped by your values. This is the fourth step, the *action* when you take control of your media consumption. The more often you practice the Empowerment Spiral, the more media savvy you become.

The Virtual Tour

Listed below are some suggestions for viewing media. As you watch television, go to the movies, rent DVDs, spend time surfing the Internet, take a walk with an iPod, or experiment with text messaging, you will move out of a world dominated by words into a world canvassed by images. Question everything. Stay awake. The kingdom of God is closer than you think.

Spiritual Exercises

Beginning with this chapter and continuing throughout the rest of the book, additional activities and resources will be available online at the Paulist Press website.

To access the online materials, go to the Paulist Press home page at www.paulistpress.com. In the search field enter: "Catechesis in a Multimedia World". Choose: "Title" in the drop-down menu. Click the "Search" button and follow the prompts to access the online activities for each chapter. You can also access the activities link by entering "Mary Byrne Hoffmann" in the search field and choosing: "Author" in the drop-down menu.

In this book, a brief description of the online material is provided within the chapters and will be located in a gray box. You can do as many of the exercises as you would like to do. Remember, the objective is for you to be immersed in the media culture. So take your time. Use the tools of the Empowerment Spiral to become more aware of your experience of media. Use your journal to jot down your thoughts.

1. Media Reflection: *WALL-E* (Rated G, 2008)

WALL-E (short for Waste Allocation Load Lifter Earth-Class) is the unlikely hero of this far-fetched but likable fable about redemption, love, and new life at the hands of a robotic tin-can garbage disposal unit. What makes the movie so fascinating is that the first part of the story is told with images only. Not one word is spoken. Watch the first twenty minutes of the movie and describe your experience of the imaged story in your journal. What story is being told? What emotions did it evoke in you?

2. Sounding Off: A Media Meditation

This is a simple exercise in media awareness. Sit comfortably in front of the television set. Turn off the sound. Experience what is being communicated only by images. Try doing this for a minimum of ten minutes. You can change channels whenever you wish. At the conclusion of the exercise, reflect on this experience almost as you might remember images in a dream.

Create three vertical columns in your journal. In the first column, list those TV images that stand out in your memory. In the next column, note your emotional response to each image. In the third column, observe if there is any correlation between the images on your list and any thoughts, feelings, or events in your personal life. Do you recognize that there is a visceral response to what you see and feel in the media experience that is often not processed or articulated but is, nonetheless, a powerful influence on viewers?

3. Online Media Reflection: *Places in the Heart*

Places in the Heart (Rated PG, 1984) is a poignant story of a young widow determined to save her cotton farm in the 1930s. Evaluate the sacramental nature of the film through a series of reflection questions.

4. Journal Exercise

In moving from images to words, where was your resistance? Where were the surprises? How is your experience of the image world different than the print world? Spend some time reflecting on what you learned from this media immersion.

7
The Sacred Encounter

You've always had the power to return home.
—*Glinda, the Good Witch,* The Wizard of Oz

The deepest desire of every pilgrim is to return home. Dorothy wants to go back to Kansas. Ulysses undergoes twenty years of trials and tribulations in his quest to return to Ithaca. Jesus, who modeled the Way, rose from the dead to return to his place with the Creator.

A few steps back in this pilgrimage, you were encouraged to find your treasure, for "there your heart will be also." The treasure that Jesus promises is a place called home. It is not a physical place. It is the fulfillment of our most primal and enduring yearning to return to an inner sense of connection and unity with ourselves, with one another, with all creation, and with the Source who is God.

THERE'S NO PLACE LIKE HOME

Where, you might ask, is home for the media pilgrim? Think about why you picked up this book. Perhaps, you were feeling disconnected from your students who seem to mumble the language of another planet. Perhaps, you sensed that traditional material and methods alone are not sufficient to reach today's youth culture. Maybe, you are already media savvy but uncertain of how to link media and faith into a more integrated catechetical approach.

There is a common theme to all these concerns: a sense of being disconnected; of not relating to either the material, the methods, the media, or the students; and of not being able to significantly relate the teachings of the Gospel to the messages of mass media.

Listen to the language of your heart's desire. What you are seeking is what every pilgrim seeks: connection, direction, clarity, and unity. Your wish to be more at home with your students, your teaching, your faith, and the world you live in is your "yellow brick road." It leads directly to where Dorothy stands, as do you, on a bridge between two worlds.

In Chapter 5, you began the journey from the familiar place of gospel tradition. In Chapter 6, you entered the unknown territory of the media culture. Moving from words to images and then images to words, you have begun to negotiate two powerful currents of human expression. Is there a meeting point for the media pilgrim where the two worlds of gospel truth and media merge to show us the way home to a better understanding of catechesis today?

THE DIVINE ENCOUNTER

The answer lies, as it did with Dorothy, within us. In the sacred tradition of pilgrimage, the meeting place of the material and spiritual worlds is the place of Divine encounter. The

Irish have a wonderful name for this meeting point. They call it "the thin place" where the veil between the two worlds is lifted to allow the pilgrim to stand on the threshold of the two realities. Of course, Christianity has another name for this encounter between the human and the divine natures: Jesus the Christ who images both God and humankind.

The key word here is *image*. The way to the realm of God in the gospel stories is lined with the images of the parables. Hopefully, in the previous chapters you have discovered that the images of television, movies, and the Internet can also pave the way to a deeper understanding of the Gospel today. Images communicate the invisible to and through the visible world. They are symbols of what is hidden and mysterious. That is why the media pilgrimage is the symbolic way. The symbolic way is the bridge that connects the world of Gospel with the world of media. Pierre Babin makes this path an imperative for catechesis.

> Do you want to express the Gospel today? Use symbolic language. That was Jesus' language, and it is the dominant language of the media today. Do you want to reveal the God of the heavens, the one who "dwells in inaccessible light"? Take the symbolic way. That was Jesus' method with his disciples.[1]

THE POWER OF IMAGES

Through images, the symbolic way returns us to the presence of God. Like Dorothy, we have always had the power to return home. Dorothy clicks her heels and says three times, "There is no place like home." We return to the Source by resourcing the image of God that resides in all of us. When we image God, we imagine a universe of Goodness. When we imagine a universe of Goodness, we participate in the continuing creation of the world. When we continue the work of creation, we are mirroring the Divine Imagination that breathes into the universe every second. We are in the presence of the Holy Mystery. We are in sacred space. We have encountered the Divine encountering us. We speak to one another in the language of the soul—images.

This place where we meet God is timeless. It is speechless. The power of image is that it speaks to what is beyond words. To what cannot be contained or limited by words. To mystery. Images don't communicate facts; they *mediate* experience. Can any doctrine possibly express the relationship between Mary and her son, Jesus, in a more intimate and moving way than Michelangelo's *Pietà*? When you are in the presence of the *Pietà*, you experience the profound sorrow of a mother for her dying son. The image touches your own experience and moves it into the bigger picture of our shared experiences. Images move us from personal understanding to communal wisdom. Is this not the meaning of the image of the Body of Christ?

Classroom Exercise: How Images Speak

Here's a good example of the effect of image on learning. After we watch a movie in my classroom, we never move to discussion. Images enter the doorway to our souls not to our heads. I don't want my students to move too quickly out of that premium space.

Instead of using words, students draw. When we finish watching *Antwone Fisher* (a heroic story of a young man's search to discover his true self against great odds), the students are asked to create a symbol that represents the message of the movie. The images are always so compelling and complete that the follow-up discussion seems hollow and unnecessary. What is even more astounding is how many students draw the same few symbols. They get it. No words.

A New Way of Seeing

Jesus understood the spirituality of images when he painted pictures with his parables. Every director, producer, writer, and marketing person in the media industry bets that you will be mesmerized by the wizardry and multiplicity of cinematic images. The bottom line is that all storytellers know that image always provides a new way of seeing that leads to a new way of being. Hollywood calls this a trend; Faith calls it transformation.

The Last Step

When you recognize that spiritual transformation in our time means bridging the images of faith and media, you are on your way home to a new understanding of catechesis and culture. By discovering what Gospel and media have in common, you begin the next part of the book with a fresh perspective of the core question. Is it possible that media, with its mixed bag of values, can be a vehicle for faith formation?

Spiritual Exercises

1. Finding Goodness in All Things

Pick a night to watch a variety of television programs—news, sitcom, drama, or reality show—or to surf the Web. How do these programs (including the commercials) and websites affirm or contradict the notion that we are made in the image of God? Can you connect any of the media messages to stories in scripture or your lesson plans?

2. Online: Made in the Image of God

Ready to try Facebook? For directions and suggestions, go to the online activities link at www.paulistpress.com (see pages 43 and 44 in this book for instructions on how to access this link).

3. Movie Reflection

Try the movie reflection exercise described in this chapter. Watch a movie or video on YouTube (www.youtube.com). Afterward in your journal, create a drawing or graphic (you might even consider a collage) that visualizes the message of the movie.

8
Transformation: A View from the Bridge

There's no place like home!
—*Dorothy*, The Wizard of Oz

He took the blind man by the hand and led him out of the village; and when he had put saliva on his eyes and laid his hands on him, he asked him, "Can you see anything?"
—*Mark 8:23*

Throughout the New Testament, Jesus restores sight to those who are blind. He gives "new eyes" to the one who could not see and, simultaneously, to all who witness and then look upon Jesus with "new eyes" of recognition. He is revealed as the One who has been sent by God. In this Divine encounter, they catch a glimmer of home "right in their own backyard."

The restoration of sight is not just a miracle that happened two thousand years ago. On a symbolic level, Jesus was giving us an important clue. When we seek to find God as we often do "somewhere over the rainbow," we embark on the way to the Way only to find at the end of the journey that God is right here, within us, in this world and indeed has been all the time. All we need to do is to wake up from our delusion that God/love/home is somewhere else. Jesus took on flesh and blood and walked this earth to image our calling: to engage the world in order to transform the world. This is essentially the work of incarnation to which we are all called where "God encounters us, communicates with us, and transforms us."[1]

Standing on the bridge that connects faith and media, "Can you see anything?" After making the media pilgrimage, do you have "new eyes"? Have you discovered the presence of God in the media culture? Do you see the interconnection of Gospel and media? Do you have renewed perspective of your ministry as a catechist in the multimedia culture?

The gift of sight is vision. The responsibility of vision is action. In every Divine encounter, we are transformed and commissioned to go forth and serve. The privilege of the Divine encounter is that we are transformed. Jesus comes out of the desert triumphant over the demons and begins his ministry. The disciples witness the ascension of Jesus into heaven only to be sent forth by the Spirit on Pentecost to begin their ministry. Where, media pilgrim, are you being sent?

The answer is, of course, that you are being sent into the world to form the spiritual lives of your students. Faith formation is the work of spiritual transformation. Your ministry is to engage your students in the world of mass media through the context of faith: To use the world, just as Jesus did, to reveal the sacred. This means not only that you filter media messages through gospel values; but it also demands that you engage media to preach the Gospel.

WHERE YOU'VE BEEN

Part One of this book was an immersion experience into the wonderful world of media. Hopefully, you have discovered how Gospel and media both share the ability to reveal what is sacred through image. Just in case you are still dangling on the edge of disbelief, I offer some words from Sr. Rose Pacatte, FSP, who links catechesis to media. Explaining that the meaning of catechesis is "to make an echo," Pacatte observes that "media provide the perfect space for that echo, that joyful noise telling salvation's story, to resound with the proclamation of the Word rooted in the experience of young people today."[2]

WHERE YOU'RE GOING

Knowing what is good and indeed holy about the image culture, the next step is to take a closer look at media. Media can indeed transform and form, and it can also fail miserably at that task. Part Two of this book is a practical workshop on filtering and creating media messages in the context of faith. It questions the values of mass media without negating the validity of its storytelling. It challenges you to take a critical look at particular media without rejecting the entire media culture. The goal of the next section is to provide you with practical tools and skills for evaluating media messages. The objective is for you to then pass these tools and skills onto your students so that they can negotiate and transform their world as informed persons of faith.

Spiritual Exercises

Before moving onto Part Two, take some time to savor your pilgrimage. Sit quietly with your journal for twenty minutes and write about your experiences with media. How do you feel at the end of this journey? Where was your resistance? Where was your delight? What was the unknown for you? Did you discover something new about media? Have you discovered the presence of God in the media culture? Did you encounter the Gospel on a deeper level more connected to the world today? Do you have a renewed perspective of your ministry as a catechist in the multimedia culture?

Part Two:
Media Ministry

9
A Guide to Part Two

This section of the book provides you with hands-on activities and resources to integrate media into your catechetical curriculum. There are two sets of activities in most chapters:

1. Interspersed throughout each chapter are exercises that provide practical ways to implement media literacy concepts in your classroom. As in Part One, some of the activities are described in the text while others can be accessed online at www.paulistpress.com. These activities are intended to foster general media awareness as it relates to fundamental issues of Christian spirituality.
2. The Tool Boxes at the end of Chapters 11 through 15 are designed to link media activities to specific topics in a spiral catechetical curriculum. For example, the Tool Box in Chapter 11 includes television, film, and internet activities that correspond to some aspect of revelation.

Here are some suggestions on how best to implement the activities:

- Don't get overwhelmed. The activities are options to help you gradually work media into your lesson plans. Pick one activity a week and enjoy the new experience.

- View all media prior to use in the classroom.
- Don't panic if media technology terms feel like a foreign language. Go to www.techterms.com for definitions.
- When possible, do the activities yourself in advance, so you have an idea of what works and what doesn't for your class.
- Unless otherwise indicated, it is recommended that the students write their responses to the exercises in their journals before sharing them in a general discussion. This gives students time to assess their individual reflections and participate more comfortably and confidently in a group discussion.
- Feel free to adapt the activities to the grade level or needs of your students. For example, when an activity calls for students to write in their journals, younger students can participate through a simple discussion.

When in doubt, remember the fourfold task of media awareness for catechists:

1. To evaluate media through the gospel lens;
2. To tell gospel stories through media;
3. To make the connections between faith and culture; and
4. To dignify human life in the media culture.

If you keep in mind that the goal of the activities is to accomplish one or more of these tasks, you will successfully move catechesis into the twenty-first century.

10
Media Ministry

> As the Spirit helped the prophets of old to see the divine plan in the signs of their times, so today the Spirit helps the Church interpret the signs of our times and carry out its prophetic tasks, among which the study, evaluation, and right use of communications technology and the media of social communications are now fundamental.
> —Aetatis Novae, *1992*

FROM PILGRIMAGE TO MINISTRY

As returning media pilgrims you have bridged the chasm between the realm of Gospel and the world of media. In the next part of your journey, you will learn how to apply the insights of the media pilgrimage to your catechetical program. You leave the pilgrim's path for the catechist's classroom. You lay down your backpack for a tool belt with the nuts and bolts to build the bridge that will bring catechesis into the twenty-first century where the children are waiting.

And they are not just waiting. They are crying for help. When I first began teaching a course on faith and media over ten years ago, students were very defensive about "their" media. Any critique was perceived as a critical statement on their culture and off limits. Now when I ask for their input on developing discussion topics for the course, media are right up there with relationships and sex. Only this time they are bashing the media. When asked to describe how media shape their values, their responses are almost uniformly negative. Media are all about "money, sex, drugs, violence." Today's media savvy generation is cynical and wary of all media messages.

This new sense of media among teens is not a victory for parents and teachers. On the contrary, it points out the urgency of our ministry to connect media messages to gospel messages. Ironically, their cynicism of the media has not reduced their consumption of the media. After all, it is the water in which they swim. Instead, they are drowning in meaninglessness and are desperate for a lifeline.

> ***Online Activity: Values Chart***
> ***Grades 1–12***
>
> Objective: To have students become aware of what is meaningful in their lives by identifying and evaluating who and/or what shapes their values.

MEDIA LITERACY TO THE RESCUE

Media literacy—the ability to read, evaluate, and create media messages—is the lifeline to future generations of responsible citizens and responsive persons of faith. It is more than a new way of teaching; it is a way of perceiving the twenty-first-century reality of a pervasive electronic media and information technology culture.

Media literacy first surfaced in Great Britain and Russia in the 1920s. However, it was during the 1960s that media literacy assumed the mantle of a movement to counter a perceived global pandemic: The worldwide exportation and infiltration of American media. France, Australia, New Zealand, and Canada (to name just a few countries) became concerned that their indigenous cultures were being infected with an American consumer values virus. As an antidote, they began developing a mandatory media literacy curriculum for elementary and secondary school students. The operative premise of the relief effort was that the proliferation of mass media was quickly moving western civilization out of the print age and into the media age. Their objective was to provide students with the critical viewing skills necessary to "read" the media for the kind of information that formerly was the privy of print. Hence, the term "media literacy."

While media literacy was enthusiastically welcomed and integrated into educational philosophies abroad, here in the United States it was initially greeted as an unwelcome intruder into the already endangered core curriculum of the 3 "Rs." Exasperated teachers unable to successfully engage the increasingly shortened attention span of their students could not imagine a solution that called for an entirely new and non-traditional approach to teaching. For almost thirty years, media literacy was a relatively unknown and misunderstood concept in American education. The most common misconception was that a media-literate curriculum was an abdication of serious teaching by turning the classroom into a movie theater. In fact, nothing could be further from the truth. Media literacy, now called "twenty-first-century learning" in academic circles, is a proven pedagogical approach to teaching and learning in an environment dominated by a growing variety of media forms now legitimized as curriculum resources.

> *Online Activity: World Watch*
> *Grades 3–12*
>
> Objective: To step "outside the box" of American media by experiencing different media perspectives from around the world.

THE CHURCH RESPONDS

Into the fray of confusion over who was to blame and what was to be done to jump-start academic participation and intellectual curiosity in our schools, a voice in the wilderness was heard. In 1977, Sr. Liz Thoman began a lifelong mission to convince American educators that media literacy was imperative. Decades in advance of the now emerging twenty-first-century learning, Sr. Liz saw the writing on the chalkboard: If children are learning differently, then we need to be teaching differently. In 1989, she founded the Center for Media Literacy (CML) to develop tools to provide teachers and catechists with the resources to integrate media literacy across curricula. In 1993, the National Catholic Educational Association (NCEA) joined with CML to create *Catholic Connections to Media Literacy*, a user-friendly primer for navigating the media culture within the context of faith. During the 1990s, dioceses across the country invited consultants from the Center to present in-service workshops on media literacy. This foundational work was supported by the United States Conference of Catholic Bishops (USCCB) and the Vatican[1]. To its credit, the Catholic Church responded to the shift from print to media consciousness in much the same way it seized new opportunities for catechesis at the beginning of the print age.

> *Online Activity: And Now a Word from Our Church*
> *Grades 6–12*
>
> Objective: To introduce the perspective of the Catholic Church on the media culture.

A VISION FOR THE FUTURE

In its most recent publication, *Literacy for the 21st Century*, the Center continues to call for educators to respond to the urgent demands of the times: "If children are to be able to navigate their lives through this multimedia culture, they need to be fluent in 'reading' and 'writing' the language of images and sounds just as we have always taught them to 'read' and 'write' the language of printed communications."[2] To the question of how teachers can do this, the Center responds:

> Schools and classrooms must be transformed from being storehouses of knowledge to being more like portable tents providing a shelter and a gathering place for students as they go out to explore, to question, to experiment, to discover…wise teachers realize that they do not have to be a "sage on the stage." Instead, their role is to be a "guide on

the side:" encouraging…guiding…mentoring…supporting the learning process.[3]

It is this understanding of electronic media as the primary learning vehicle that informs the Center's definition of media literacy:

> Media Literacy is a 21st-century approach to education. It provides a framework to access, analyze, evaluate, create and participate using messages in a variety of forms—from print to video to the Internet.[4]

With a bow to the work of the Center and the vision of the church, media literacy has evolved with the development of advanced communications technologies to give birth to a new generation of literacies specifically related to various media forms (e.g., digital media literacy is the ability to read, sort, analyze, synthesize and produce digital media messages). Now considered pivotal to human development, media literacy is endorsed by a long list of international organizations invested in the intellectual, mental, and emotional health of our children. (For a sampling of these organizations, see Medialiteracy.com). Throughout the world, there is a growing sense of urgency that we must prepare our children for the world that no longer awaits them but is perhaps devouring them.

WHAT A DIFFERENCE A CENTURY MAKES!

The distinctions between learning in a print culture and a media culture resonate with what many educators witness in the classroom. This comparative table of twentieth-century and twenty-first-century learning has become a conversion piece for those who doubt the necessity of a media integrated curriculum.

19th–20th Century Learning: Content Mastery	21st Century Learning: Process Skills
• Limited access to knowledge and information (i.e. "content") primarily through print • Emphasis on learning content knowledge that may or may not be used in life • Goal is to master content knowledge (literature, history, science, etc.) • Facts and information are "spoon-fed" by teachers to students • Print-based information analysis with pen-and-ink tools • Pencil/pen and paper or word processing for expression • Classroom-limited learning and dissemination with little collaboration • Textbook learning from one source, primarily print-based media • Conceptual learning on individual basis • "Lock-step" age-based exposure to content knowledge • Mastery demonstrated through papers and tests • Teacher selecting and lecturing • Teacher evaluates and assesses work and assigns grade • Teaching with state-adopted textbooks for subject area with little accountability for teaching • Students passive vessels	• Infinite access to knowledge and information (content) through Internet • Emphasis on process skills for life-long learning • Goal is to learn skills (access, analyze, evaluate, create, participate) to solve problems • Teachers use discovery approach based on a process of inquiry • Multimedia analysis and collaboration using technology tools • Powerful multimedia technology tools for expression, circulation, and dissemination • World-wide learning and connecting, with ability to team up world-wide • Real-world, real-time learning from multiple sources, using technology tools • Project-based learning on team basis • Flexible individualized exposure to content knowledge and process skills • Mastery demonstrated through multimedia • Teacher framing and guiding • Students learn to set criteria and to evaluate own work • Teaching to state education standards with testing for accountability • Students active participants and contributors

© 2008 Center for Media Literacy/www.medialit.org

> *Online Activity: Guide on the Side Experiment*
> *Grades 6–12*
>
> Objective: To give both students and teachers an experience of a collaborative learning lesson conducted by students.

MEDIA LITERACY AND CATECHESIS

The purpose of religious education and faith formation is to provide a spiritual framework for righteous living in this world. A media literate catechetical program supports that agenda with the following objectives:

- To prepare students for full participation in the world by modeling an integrated approach to life that weaves together the complementary realities of spirit and matter—Gospel and culture;
- To filter media messages in light of the Gospel in order to provide students with the tools to identify the value messages transmitted by mass media;
- To encourage responsible use of media by providing students with hands-on experience in media production;
- To provide a collaborative learning environment where non-competitive teamwork in recognition of individual skills is integral to the outcome and assessment of the learning process and to individual self-worth.

Furthermore, *Aetatis Novae*[5] speaks to the necessity of media integration in faith formation:

> Moreover, as the Church always must communicate its message in a manner suited to each age and to the cultures of particular nations and peoples, so today it must communicate in and to the emerging media culture. (#8)

> Along with traditional means such as witness of life, catechetics, personal contact, popular piety, the liturgy and similar celebrations, the use of media is now essential in evangelization and catechesis.... The media of social communications can and should be instruments in the Church's program of re-evangelization and new evangelization in the contemporary world. (#11)

> *Online Activity: Making the Connections*
> *Grades 6–12*
>
> Objective: To introduce students to the connections between the world of Gospel and the world of media.

A NEW MINISTRY FOR NEW TIMES

The call to serve in this multimedia culture of streaming info-images has created a new ministry for catechists. Your mission is to toss out the lifeline of media literacy and pull our children back into safe waters where they can navigate the often opposing currents of Gospel and culture.

This section of the book is designed to train you to be media ministers—twenty-first-century evangelists. The core concepts of media literacy will provide you with the language and the skills to create a media-based catechetical program. Through suggested lesson plans and online activities, you can explore the media landscape with your students. Together, you and your students will examine the place of faith and the church in this new cultural environment and evaluate the impact of their message and authority. You will become media literate, media fluent, and media storytellers.

> *Online Activity: Media in the Classroom*
> *Grades 1–12*
>
> Objective: To share the process of integrating media into your curriculum with your students.

THE CORE CONCEPTS OF MEDIA LITERACY

The goal of your ministry is to make sure that faith formation occurs *within* not *outside* the culture by using the tools of media literacy. Using complementing catechetical curricula, media literacy spirals through elementary and secondary curricula moving from simple to complex applications. Like the culture, it threads itself through all academic disciplines and into all manners of living. Reflecting the social networking nature of internet information gathering, it fosters collaborative learning. In particular, the media minister facilitates a participatory environment of inquiry and exploration into matters of faith.

The five core concepts of media literacy are your tools for constructing the bridge between faith and media, between print and image. Each of the following concepts will be explored within the context of gospel spirituality.

1. The audience negotiates meaning.
2. All media construct reality.
3. Media messages use a creative language with its own rules.
4. Most media are businesses organized to gain profit/power.
5. Media shape values.

When media literacy is woven into catechesis, critical thinking skills of inquiry and reflection are applied to the process of making good media choices. By holding media messages under a microscope, viewers of every age can look closely at the small but organic elements that make up the big picture.

THE MISSION AHEAD

Media ministry prepares the faithful to respond to the world of mass mediated images and messages with faith, hope, and love. In catechesis, this means evaluating how media affects not just our daily lives but our spiritual well-being. In a very real sense, the media minister is a prophet heralding a new age of spiritual and cultural reconciliation. As is often the case, the prophet must leave her/his own land in order to be heard.

You are being sent out to a foreign land with its own spiritual and cultural topography—the hearts, minds, and souls of our youth. Your mission is to venture into their wired brains and plugged-in souls to spark a connection between the media that they consume and the Gospel that we teach. In one hand you hold the Bible; in the other hand the remote control. The task of reconciliation is to reclaim the authority and wisdom of the storyteller. The first rule of every good storyteller is to know their audience. The next chapter introduces you to that audience through the first core concept of media literacy.

11
Core Concept #1: The Audience Negotiates Meaning

> Media education is "quest for meaning.... Uncovering the many levels of meaning in a media message and the multiple answers to even basic questions is what makes media education so engaging."
> —*Chris Worsnop*, Screening Images

MEDIA MINISTERS ON A MISSION

I grew up in the shadow of a Maryknoll seminary—the massive edifice of missionary training that still crowns a gentle slope overlooking the Hudson River in Ossining, New York. For as long as I can remember, *Maryknoll* magazine was a fixture on our living room coffee table. My parents had grown up in the same town with several Maryknoll missionaries who were eventually sent to the Philippines and South America. When these exotic men returned stateside, I retrieved slices of hushed adult conversation from the upper balcony seating of my second floor bedroom. Their tales inspired both the fear and fascination that fashions a life calling: I was going to be a missionary!

As it turned out, there was a slightly different, perhaps less romantic version of that plan in the wings. It was not the hinterlands of a remote continent that beckoned but the 750-channel universe of a remote consciousness. Interestingly enough, much of the wisdom that I gleaned from those long ago stolen conversations applies to the mission of the media minister to the aliens—"Digital Natives"—of the media culture. Very simply, the story that we tell is only as good as the audience we know.

Your Mission

The first thing that you need to know about your students is that they are not *you*! No one knows this better than the marketing experts who are vying for the attention of billions of young people worldwide. Their business thrives on the generation gap creating hordes of hungry consumers with growing appetites for the latest trends and products. The cultural chasm created by technology has only sent Madison Avenue into a feeding frenzy. With so many psychological and behavioral shifts in generations born after 1980, the possibilities are endless for target marketing.

The first step toward corralling the horde of potential buyers is to brand the audience by giving the targets a name. Today's marketplace is made up of a host of distinctive buyers from Baby Boomers (1946–1964) to Generation X (1965–1980) to Generation Y, also known as the Millennials (1980–1995). Straddling the generational boundaries are the Net Geners and the Digital Natives who reach across decades of technological innovation (1980–present). The new kids on the targeting block have been duly categorized and alphabetized as Generation Z (2001–present) also known as Generation We or the We Boomers—a generation that is being fed and fattened (quite literally) on an internet diet.

The names that Madison Avenue call us may be arbitrary and subject to debate. You probably don't define yourself or your children by these labels. Nevertheless, marketers are counting on you to behave and to buy according to their labels. They know something significant about human nature: We are defined by how we see the world and how the world sees us. And, the way we see ourselves varies from one generation to another. There it is again—the resilient yet fluid power of image to create a message that speaks to the audience of the moment. The challenge as catechists is to use this insight to reach your audience with a message that is timeless and yet relevant to the Net Geners, Digital Natives, and We Boomers.

> *Online Activity: Who Do They Think We Are?*
> *Grades 1–12*
>
> Objective: To make students aware of target marketing as a technique to shape consumer values and behavior in order to sell products.

1. Getting to Know Them

It may seem almost crass to think of those young souls in front of you as an audience (from the Latin *audentia* meaning "a hearing, listening") but that is exactly how they see themselves. Here are a few tips on how to keep them tuned to your message.

After years of being courted to the point of harassment by a variety of persistent media-message makers, our children are now at the mercy of the denizens of Madison Avenue and Hollywood. In fact, along with the endless array of products that they either consume or covet, they themselves have bought the image of an audience aiming to be pleased. Along with that image comes a certain set of expectations every time their attention is engaged.

- When someone speaks, they expect a performance;
- Every performance should be engaging (as in multi-sensory);
- Performances should be brief (no more than five minutes);
- Technological props (DVD players, smartboards, iPods) get and sustain their attention.

These expectations are so often met by the media culture that they have become unconscious demands that filter into every area of our children's lives including the classroom. When these expectations are not met, both teacher and students are distracted.

> ***Online Activity: Attraction or Distraction***
> ***Grades K–12***
>
> Objective: To help students become aware of the rightful place of stimulation and contemplation in their lives.

2. Understand Their Culture

Contrary to public dismay, the craving for performance over presentation in the classroom is not about entertainment. It is about engagement. Our youth live in a multimedia culture of multisensory stimulation that says, "Engage me or enrage me."[1] This is how they receive and send information. They are not to be blamed for expecting something that we perhaps cannot deliver. Our job is to place the Gospel in the context of their culture so that Gospel forms connective tissue to their reality. This means using a wide range of visual and digital resources including the Internet to make the message compelling and relevant.

> *Activity: Audience Feedback*
> *Grades 6–12*
>
> Objective: To let your students (your audience) teach you about how best to engage them.
> Have the students prepare a lesson plan using a variety of media forms: television programs, commercials, film clips, internet sites, podcasts. Have fun!

3. Get inside Their Heads

You've probably said this every time someone under the age of seven comes to the rescue of your earnest but ill-fated attempt to hook up a DVD player: "Kids today are just born with a different brain." This is no joke. The brain on Internet is wired for instant gratification. They are the point-and-click generations. Point to the website; click to the right answer.

They are used to getting information right away and without much effort. The best way to motivate them to probe beneath the surface is to create a learning environment based on inquiry. Stress questions over answers. Questions are still the prerogative of the human soul.

> *Online Activity: Question Collage*
> *Grades 4–12*
>
> Objective: To awaken your students to their life questions by working with images.

4. Travel to Their World View

It may take a village to raise a child but it takes a global village to keep her attention. The World Wide Web has eradicated natural borders. Facebook allows the Net Geners to reach out and make contact with anyone in the world. The battle cry of bigotry, "Not in my backyard" doesn't work when your backyard is the world. The Net Geners pride themselves on their global consciousness of diversity, which is the gateway to the Gospel of inclusivity. Open it. Today's students are right on the other side.

> *Online Activity: Surfing outside the Box*
> *Grades 6–12*
>
> Objective: To work with students as they explore the diversity of the web of life on the Web.

5. Speak Their Language

When you speak the language of global consciousness through media integration in your catechetical program, you and your students are both on the same planet. You have a message. You have an audience. And, most important, you have the basis for an ongoing conversation. As you will discover, media-based catechesis can become a mutual learning experience.

> *Online Activity: Switching Roles*
> *Grades 4–12*
>
> Objective: To provide an experience of collaborative teaching and learning that simultaneously allows the teacher to become an active participant in the students' culture.

6. Respect the Differences

The mission today is not about conversion; it is about connection. With their eyes glued to the screen and their fingers rapidly tapping out a text message to a remote party, the Digital Natives appear to be an isolated clan. Don't let tribal rituals fool you into false assumptions. Take another look. The Net Geners are always connected to some form of community. The big difference is that most of their communication is interactive and online. This is not about the devaluation of personal contact that they still prefer with close friends and family. It is about the expanse of possibilities offered by the great big World Wide Web out there. Is there virtue in virtual connection? Let them be your teachers. Accept them as they are—not who we were. Approach them with wonderment and judgment. They have something to tell you about this new world. They just might be prophets in their own time.

> ***Online Activity: Media Open Space***
> ***Grades 3–12***
>
> Objective: To begin a conversation with one another across the cultural chasm without shouting across the digital divide.

A COMMON BOND

Now that you know something about what distinguishes you from your audience, here's the next most important thing the media minister needs to know: The audience out there is just like *you* but in a different way. The assumption we often carry into catechesis is that student and teacher are joined at the soul with the same image of a Judeo-Christian God. When we rely on that premise, we make a dangerous leap of faith—bypassing the real connection of a common spiritual hunger. It is this longing for something bigger than ourselves that Madison Avenue contorts into a rapacious consumerism that wants and needs for something only for ourselves. What gets lost in the crowd of so many messages are the instinctive human responses to universal questions: Where did I come from? Where am I going? How and where do I find meaning? Who do I love? Am I loved? Whom do I serve? How do I see myself, others, and God in the culture that I live in? What is just? What is merciful? Why is there evil? These are the questions that bind us in our commonality and in our difference.

> *Online Activity: Questioning Media*
> *Grades 4–12*
>
> Objective: To encourage students to experience media as thought-provoking and reflective—not just entertaining and passive.

IT'S ALL IN THE DELIVERY

Intrinsic to the questions of *how* we see ourselves is the *way* we see ourselves. How are our stories delivered to us? The medium is not only the message; it determines how we negotiate meaning. This is an important distinction for the catechist who was taught in the print age and is now teaching students born and bred in the media age. The way we take in information is very different and consequently so is our world view. Apples and oranges, Boomers and Millennials, earthlings to Digital Natives—however you wish to explain the dynamic, we have a failure to communicate if we don't recognize the differences between how we learn in the print age and in the media age.

Print with its logical sequencing of word and thought and fixed position on paper maintains an objective authority. The reader, standing outside the text, uses critical thinking skills to interpret the author's message. However, image with its fluid interplay of color, shape, and feeling invites the viewer to enter into the image. The silent ambiguity of the artist's vision allows the viewer to imagine the possibilities of meaning. Unlike the printed word, which can entertain several different but limited intellectual interpretations, the image can have as many meanings as viewers.

Think of the enigma of *Mona Lisa*'s smile. Everyone who views the Da Vinci masterpiece assigns a different meaning to that mysterious expression. Is she smiling? Is she scowling? Is she mocking? What was Da Vinci's intention? The audience negotiates the possibilities of meaning through the lens of their own experience. Unlike print, image claims no external authority. Instead, image affirms the power of the beholder to negotiate meaning based on the internal authority of the viewer's own life experiences.

> ***Online Activity: The Power of Images***
> ***Grades 1–12***
>
> Objective: To make students conscious of how images communicate and how each of us can have a different perspective of the same image. This is a good tie-in to discussions about the unconscious but often damaging influence of violent and sexually inappropriate images in media.

THE NEON GLASS WINDOWS

The ambivalence of image is pretty murky territory for the catechist who teaches from scriptural authority. Mass media, with its millions of images, has hurled us off the terra firma of dogmatic certainty into the unchartered waters of visual and sensory ambiguity. As a result, we are undergoing a gradual but certain transformation in our perception of reality. The human consciousness of the media age hungers not for the assurance of facts but for the abundance of experiences. As catechists, you teach from a faith perspective that assumes that doctrine dictates meaning. Our children live in a multiplex universe where audience negotiates meaning.

The rebellion against doctrine is creating a disparity between how we tell (as teachers) and how we hear (as students) our sacred stories. Can those of us who learned by the book teach those who want to throw away the book? How does the catechist communicate the gospel message to an audience that craves meaning over message?

> *Online Activity: What's It All About?*
> *Grades 6–12*
>
> Objective: This one is for the catechists. Do you know how your students understand or even value "meaning"?

IN CONCLUSION

Media ministers have an obligation to respond to the messages of Madison Avenue by asking the big questions of identity and meaning first of ourselves and then of our students in the context of a rich tradition of spiritual inquiry. It is precisely this exercise that is the backbone of the pastoral process discussed in Chapter 6. Now we introduce that same process into our curriculum to help students recognize their unique spiritual identities and how they negotiate meaning in the information age.

THE TOOL BOX: MEDIA AND REVELATION

The following media and internet activities are designed to support your lesson plans on "revelation" as it pertains to each grade level in a spiral catechetical curriculum. The exercises invite your students to compare how meaning is found in the revealed word of sacred scripture and in the virtual images of the media culture. Unless otherwise noted, all activities can be adapted for use in grades 1 through 12.

1. Empowerment Spiral

The Empowerment Spiral had its beginnings in the Catholic Family Movement in the 1950s. Originally called the Pastoral Circle, it was later adapted by small faith communities in Latin America for the study of scripture. James and Evelyn Whitehead implemented the Circle as a tool for religious education and Joe Holland used it in the peace movement. *Catholic Connections to Media Literacy* (a joint media literacy curriculum produced by the Center for Media Literacy and the NCEA) adopted the Circle dynamics into the Empowerment Spiral. The Spiral has since been recognized as an excellent lens for filtering media messages.

The four stages of the Empowerment Spiral (see page 42) awaken students to their own reflective processing of media. In this exercise, students will focus on the question of how media support the concept of revelation as "God's self-disclosure in salvation history." As students move through the Circle, they will assess whether or not media reflect the Judeo-Christian assurance that creation is intrinsically good through the enduring presence of a loving God. The goal of this activity is to cultivate critical thinking and viewing skills in the audience. These skills when applied to all forms of electronic media will gradually encourage your students to recognize their own experience of what is meaningful in today's culture.

Preparation

a. Select a scripture passage related to the inquiries of revelation (Who made me? How do we come to know God? How do we respond to God? How do we encounter God?) to be read aloud or assigned for reading depending on the age of the group. (For example, the Creation story in Genesis.)

b. Suggest an age-appropriate television program or movie that complements the scripture passage.
(Suggested time frame: 1 to 2 lessons. You may want to have the students show a scene from their selected programs. In that case, you will need at least two days for this activity. Be sure that you screen all programs in advance.)

Stage 1: Awareness

Ask the students to describe their experience of listening to/reading the scripture passage and of watching the television program? How did it make them feel?

(Try to elicit an emotional response in this part. All you want is a visceral reaction to the text or program. Example: "The Bible story was boring" or "The cartoon made me laugh.")

Stage 2: Analysis

Ask students why the passage and the TV show made them feel a certain way.

(Try to get the students to make associations here. Why do you think the scripture story was boring? Had you heard it before? What was the boring part? Why do you think that the TV program was more interesting?)

Stage 3: Reflection

This is when you begin to connect the dots between Gospel and culture using the questions in the revelation curriculum. Depending on your scripture and media selections and the age group, ask students to compare how the two mediums answer basic inquiries regarding God's existence, our creation, the human-divine relationship, our encounter with God in daily living. Many of them will be surprised that it is possible to discover "gospel truth" on television or in the movies! Some suggested questions for students: What is the scripture story saying about God's presence in the world? How about the TV show? What are the similarities and differences in the storytelling? How do the stories reflect your experience of God's presence in your life and the world around you?

Stage 4: Action

Discuss with your class if (and then how) this exercise has changed their experience of both scripture and media. Can they see how media really are telling some of the same stories that are found in scripture? Is there a different sense of God in scripture and media? How has this exercise affected their sense of God? For the older students: How has it affected their sense of culture? Has it enhanced their appreciation of scripture?

2. Drawing Conclusions

After watching any kind of visual media in class, go for the gut reaction before the articulated response. In those first few moments after the screen goes dark, most of us are in a dreamlike state. The experience of the movie or program has yet to work its way up to the cerebral cortex. It is, instead, raw emotion, making us sad or happy or angry or confused. This is not the time for words. This is the time to bring out the crayons and speak the language of images. (This is a more extended version of a similar spiritual exercise for catechists in Part One.)

Preparation

Choose a film that relates to how God continues to be revealed in our times. View the film without interruption and comment. At the end of the film, ask the students to respond to the following questions with images. You can use these questions for any grade level. It is very important that the teacher presents his/her own example of the suggested drawings:

a. How did the movie make you feel? Students can either draw a picture of something that makes them feel the same way the movie did or just use colors to represent their feelings. (Example: A student who feels good after watching the movie might draw a sunny sky.)

b. Draw a symbol or image that represents the message of the movie as it relates to an aspect of revelation. One option is to have some magazines available for the students to create a visual collage that captures the essence of the movie.

Presentation

Allow time for students to present and interpret their drawings. Your main task is to keep the conversation focused and to integrate your important points about revelation into the discussion.

Film Suggestions

You can check out reviews for most movies with Catholic News Service: http://www.catholicnews.com/movies.htm.

- *Finding Nemo* (Rated G, elementary school): God's steadfast and persistent love.
- *The Spitfire Grill* (Rated PG-13, middle school/high school): The presence of Christ in the least among us.
- *Finding Forrester*: (Rated PG-13, high school): God continuing the work of creation and transformation through human beings.

---

3. Online: Facebook Gets a Facelift

In Chapter 7, page 51, you were encouraged to create your own Facebook page. Are you ready to bring Facebook into the classroom? Go online and check out some suggestions for Facebook activities related to your lesson plans on revelation.

12
Core Concept #2: All Media Construct Reality

> I am the Creator—of a television show that gives hope and joy and inspiration to millions.
> —*Christof, a character in* The Truman Show

> I am the way, and the truth, and the life.
> —*John 14:6,
> words spoken by Jesus Christ that for 2,000 years
> have given "hope and joy and inspiration to millions."*

THE LIFE AND TIMES OF TRUMAN

Hollywood can't resist a good story even if it means debunking its own mythology. In 1998, *The Truman Show*, starring comedian Jim Carrey, startled critics, audience, and the film industry alike with its pointed jab at the media bubble. Busting the hype that mass media reflects reality, *The Truman Show* told a story of something much more complex and cynical. In the process, it asked the kind of questions about our culture usually reserved for theologians and philosophers.

In this modern day fable of self-discovery, Truman, the happiest man in the town of Seahaven, slowly and painfully discovers that he is living in the completely fabricated world of a reality show in which he has unwittingly been the star since birth. As we watch him and his perfect world disintegrate under the burden of deceit, the parallels between his mediated reality and our media culture are unsettling.

WHAT'S THE BIG REAL?

The good news is that the kids today, unlike Truman, don't believe that anything they see on TV or in the movies or on the Internet is real. The bad news is that many of those same kids don't think anything that they read in the Gospels is real, either. The perennial philosophical question: What is real? treads shallow water these days. The answer, if you ask any kid glued to a video game, is "nothing." Negotiating meaning means negotiating reality. If nothing is real, then where is the meaning? That's the problem.

MEDIA CONSTRUCT REALITY

It is true that nothing we see on television or in the movies is "real"—not even the news. All media construct reality through the manipulation of perspective, content, and inevitably audience. Media are always someone else's idea (not yours) of what is happening, what/who is of value, what/who is expendable. Media makers—directors, producers, writers, editors, 24/7 cable news commentators, and Comedy Central "news anchors" Jon Stewart and Stephen Colbert—are modern-day storytellers. They are sometimes brilliant and insightful, even visionary. They are sometimes mundane, mediocre, and inflammatory. However, they are all primarily interested in constructing a story that will attract an audience by doing all the same things that storytellers have done throughout time. They embellish the plot, make the characters either larger or smaller than life, dress up the ordinary with extraordinary effects, and masterfully pull at our emotional strings. However, unlike the print culture, today's media provide us with the pictures and sounds that used to reside in our imagination. Add to this the fact that media are all day, all night, everywhere. It is just a slippery slope into the perception that media mirror life, life mirrors media, and if media are not real, then neither is life.

> *Online Activity: Life as a Sitcom or Not!*
> *Grades 4–12*
>
> Objective: To filter media reality by drawing the distinctions between real life and real media; to use media as an occasion to look inside oneself instead of just outside to the screen. (For younger children, I recommend using a cartoon and, of course, keeping the discussion simple.)

THE DANGER WITHIN

The Net Geners—most of the students we teach—are just fine making the unconscious leap from media to life to media without making distinctions. In some ways, that is their reality. With the touch or a click, they change their experiences constantly and at will. Reality gets edited, reformatted, revised, mashed-up, and deleted. The manipulation of images and words creates an unsettling sense of impermanence that can lead to apathy. Like Truman they are trapped in a world without awareness.

What is missing from their consciousness is the wonderfully ironic relativity of metaphor. Their point-click-play-pause-stop-rewind-delete world provides a safe haven of control and therefore cocky self-centered certainty. As Mike Hayes comments, "The result is a world that young adults live in where they expect answers that are simple, clear-cut and require little thought."[1] What they don't see are all the self-appointed Christofs of the media world—the people behind the controls creating a false reality and selling it as the real thing. Out of sight and out of mind, these silent stalkers of hearts and minds provide a barrage of vicarious experiences to distract curiosity and contemplation.

The constructed reality of big screens and palm screens has the very real potential to obscure the underlying truth of the big picture: Human beings question. Our deep and often unresolved longing to know what is real inspires both fear and faith. Out of that tension and uncertainty come more questions. And so the human soul evolves. The danger of the quick and easy answers coupled with the intoxication of experience over the sobriety of reflection is that it can induce a spiritual coma. The nature of mass media to shape a pervasive material reality can simultaneously threaten the intrinsic response of human beings to question that reality.

SO, WHOSE REALITY IS IT, ANYWAY?

In a culture where truth is perhaps irrelevant, what is the media minister to do? How do we transmit the enduring reality of the gospel message in a cultural environment of personalized customized realities?

The first solution is to remember that your mission is to awaken your students to the very real and profound experience of their spirituality. Without diminishing the value of media experiences, the media minister needs to suggest the clarifying balance of transcendent experiences. That is, you need to subvert the superficial certainty of a point-click culture with the symbolic language of faith.

> *Online Activity: Internet Fast*
> *Grade Level: Anyone who uses the Internet*
>
> Objective: To give students "time out" from the digital world so that they can "tune in" to the symbolic world of their own incredible, curious souls!

A CASE IN POINT

The urgency of facilitating transcendent experiences was shockingly brought home to me recently while viewing the PBS documentary *Growing Up Online*[2] with my students. Over and over again, the film made the point that the digital culture of immediate answers and information overload was somehow numbing reflective impulses. To the one, the students unequivocally agreed. Just to be sure that their patent disinterest was not a function of some misunderstanding, I rattled off a sampling of questions related to faith, morals, and meaning and asked if they considered these questions to be important. My heart sunk as they simply shrugged their shoulders with boredom and dismissal.

Later that same week, I happened to come across a television interview with Eric Schmidt, Chairman and CEO of Google, Inc., that corroborated the students' response. When asked how children today are adjusting to digital technology, he responded with some concern. "I worry that the level of interrupt, the sort of overwhelming rapidity of information—and especially of stressful information—is in fact affecting cognition. It is in fact affecting deeper thinking."[3] Unfortunately, many teachers who are witnessing a similar resistance to abstract thinking and contemplative reflecting would not disagree.

> *Online Activity: Be Still and Know*
> *Grades K–12*
>
> Objective: To change the energy of the traditional classroom where right answers rule the day to the energy of spiritual intuition where wisdom offers quiet counsel.

A SOLUTION

In an impromptu conversation on a staff retreat, Brother Don Bisson, FMS, a renowned Jungian scholar and retreat leader on contemporary spiritual issues, listened patiently as I recounted the *Growing Up Online* experience with my students. To my surprise, he did not suggest the obvious remedy of injecting the course with a good shot of faith but instead prescribed a strong dose of doubt—the kind of subversive cultural dislocation that is at the heart of the gospel message. As discussed in Chapter 5, Jesus used parables and miracles to turn the world of his followers upside down and inside out. He brought them into another dimension where all things that are impossible are made possible. The lame walk. The blind see. The prodigal son is forgiven. Jesus planted the seeds of doubt in the fertile darkness of what is known in order to nurture faith in what is unknown.

The leap from the known to the unknown, from the possible to the impossible is a transcendent experience. As catechists in the twenty-first century, your challenge is to lead your students from the precipice of their certainty to the brink of their disbelief. Rock their digital media world! Challenge their assumptions about reality. Find out what they believe in. Ask them what they find hard to believe. Encourage them to make the journey into the impossible otherness of life.

MEDIA AS SUBVERSIVE

Media provides many opportunities for transcendence. It is just a matter of discovering those moments with your students. What is the symbolic equivalent of the mustard seed, the lost sheep, the pearl of great value in their stories? What carries the astonishing implausibility of healing the sick, walking on water, feeding thousands with mere crumbs? Where is the doorway into the impossible, unbelievable, miraculous? Where does the ordinary become the extraordinary? Both Karl Rahner and Evelyn Underhill—the theologian and the mystic—believed that spirituality is grounded in everyday experiences. If they were alive and counseling us now, they would most assuredly suggest that everyday media are an occasion of faith.

The media minister has the subversive power to shape a reality where the Gospel is found in popular culture at the same time that the Gospel is used to question popular culture. You use the media to make the Gospel relevant: You use the Gospel to make the media pertinent. You reclaim your authority as teacher, preacher, and parent—jobs both hijacked by and then surrendered to the media. You stand between the media and the audience and filter the messages. You become storytellers again speaking in the symbolic language of faith to restore a "yearning for the unbounded."[4]

THE TOOL BOX: MEDIA, GOSPEL, AND REALITY

The following activities focus on how media images and stories reflect the realities of both the Trinity and the person of Jesus Christ.

1. TV and the Trinity

The Trinity is an essential truth and an unfathomable mystery of the Catholic faith. We, who are created in the image of God, all embody the attributes of the Trinity. We create through love. We redeem our lives and those around us through the healing graces of forgiveness and compassion. We are, by the very nature of our inherent goodness, a sanctified people who seek lives of holiness. How does the tale of this wonderful mystery unravel in the characters and stories of primetime TV?

a. Define what it means to create, redeem, and sanctify. Ask students to provide examples from their personal experience.
b. Have students find characters in media that do the work of the Trinity—creating, redeeming, sanctifying. Bring media examples into the class for presentation.

If we experience the Trinity in the media and in our lives, is it really such a mystery?

2. The Way

Jesus says: "I am the way, and the truth, and the life." This is a twofold task:

a. How does Jesus show us the Way in the following actions?
   - Being a good friend or sibling
   - Following the Beatitudes
   - Living the Great Commandment
   - Responding to the needs of the world (right relationship)
b. Using the same list, select stories from a variety of media that reinforce or undermine these same actions.

3. Online: Jesus Goes to the Movies
A Reflection on *The Truman Show*
Grades 9–12

Objective: To discover the continuing story of Jesus the Christ in contemporary media by identifying the parallels between the story of Truman and the life of Jesus.

4. Online: Modern Day Parables on the Internet
Catechists

Here comes YouTube! It had to happen sooner or later. First, you took a peek at YouTube in Part One. Now, it's time to bring YouTube into the classroom. Go to the activities link for suggestions on how to use YouTube appropriately with your students.

13
Core Concept #3: Media Messages Use a Creative Language with Its Own Rules

> A Christian communicator cannot put forward a message nowadays if he or she does not engage the affective life of the group. And if faith is not made affectively desirable, it is difficult to manifest faith.[1]
>
> —*Pierre Babin*

MAY I HAVE YOUR ATTENTION, PLEASE?

It is one thing to tell a story; it is quite another thing to captivate an audience. In another time and place, the teacher might reach into her bag of tricks to command attention. Today, that reach is across a chasm that separates the bells and whistles of a bygone era from the special effects of an entertainment culture addicted to multisensory engagement. Calibrated to the ten-second byte, the brain of the Net Geners wants and needs to be stimulated right now and as often as possible. Take a good look at your audience. They are waiting for something that you cannot give them—the emotional jolt of special effects: screeching car chases, spine-chilling music, suggestive camera angles, the prompt of laugh tracks, pixilated animation, the incredible magic of computer graphics.

Special effects are the languages that the media use to communicate powerful nonverbal messages. They are crafted illusory and multisensory prompts—audio, visual, and digital—intended to provoke the imagination. In the image culture of mass media, special effects are narrative guides that stage the story for the audience. The close-up of a personal encounter draws the audience into the intimate moment. A sudden shift in the sound track anticipates a change in mood and prepares the audience for a happy ending or tragic turn of events. (Decades after the *Jaws* trilogy, is it safe to go back in the water?) Unlike books and lectures, these messages do not speak to the mind; they awaken the body. Also called "emoticons," special effects do not transmit facts; they trigger emotions. They do not provide lessons; they offer experience. Without benefit of a word, the language of sounds and images completely engages the senses. In the middle of an intergalactic battle scene in *Star Wars*, no one had to ask the audience for attention.

> *Online Activity: Touch the Sound*
> *Grades 1–12*
>
> Objective: To experience the intrinsic ability of sound to tell a story and provoke emotional responses. This exercise will make believers of your students.

Magic or Mystery

It is ironic that catechists are losing their audience to the thrill of special effects. Just open up your Bible and a tale will be told marked by the spectacular—from the burning bush to the Virgin birth to the resurrection. Take another look at Matthew and read the subheadings in each chapter: Jesus Cleanses a Leper; Jesus Stills a Storm; Jesus Heals a Paralytic; Jesus Walks on Water. The gospel tradition is not lacking in its share of awe-inspiring, gasp-producing moments. You might justifiably counter that the difference between what we see in the visual media is different than what we read in the Bible. And you would be half right. Special effects in movies are props designed to construct a reality. Special effects in the Bible are miracles meant to reflect a reality. However, there is something that both media and Gospel have in common: the affect of the effect on our sense of reality.

> ### *Online Activity: A World of Special Effects*
> ### *Grades 1–12*
>
> Objective: To give students an experience of how special effects in nature help to tell the story of God's creation.

Good News

In the end, it does not matter how you get your special effects—whether you read about them, see them, hear them—as long as you experience them.

Let's go back to the Gospels. It certainly matters to us what Jesus said two thousand years ago. We continue to teach, preach, and study his words. As discussed in Chapter 4, the early church was as much captivated by how Jesus made them feel as by what he said. When biblical scholars ponder the rapid movement of the Gospel throughout the Middle East and into Asia Minor, especially given the circumstances of Jesus' death, they often cite the inclusivity of his message as the integral growth factor. The "special effects" of his miracles had the affect of making his followers feel visible, cleansed, included, loved, forgiven, indeed whole human beings. That message of inclusivity and visibility and how it made people feel caught the attention of all who witnessed or heard it. It was good news for people who were never considered anything other than bad news. Good news has a way of getting around.

> *Online Activity: A Gospel of Special Affects*
> *Grades 3–12*
>
> Objective: To experience how special effects in the New Testament affect our connection to the person of Jesus today.

OUR MESSAGE

We need more affect in our faith formation. We don't need special effects. We have them in scripture and in our rituals—incense, holy water, the sacraments, the Mass, Gregorian chant, vespers and novenas, prayer and meditation. All of these sacred elements of our tradition have the same desired effect of allowing us to experience the underlying meaning of the ritual or the gesture. In other words, to open ourselves to all that is holy and enter into the presence of the Divine.

What we need to ask ourselves: Are we teaching or are we facilitating this experience? Have we turned the special effects of our tradition into a lesson plan instead of a religious experience? We have a story to tell about a man who was both human and divine. This, in and of itself, is an incredible "special effect." The purpose of the incarnation was to demonstrate how we can live more fully as human beings in relationship with God in this world. A relationship has to be experienced; it cannot be taught. Like the media culture that we live in, living the Gospel is a multisensory event full of unprecedented spectacular effects that affect the way we see ourselves, one another, and God.

As inheritors of a rich spiritual tradition, we know that moments of wonder are readily available to us. Are we making them readily available to our students, or should they seek them instead only in the silence and darkness of a movie theater?

THE TOOL BOX: MEDIA AND SACRAMENTS

Transcendence begins by tuning your audience into and onto the special affects of the sacramental in all dimensions of human life. The following activities will guide you in this important sensory engagement by using media to enhance your discussion of the sacraments. As you will see, the exercises allow your students to witness the sanctity of God's presence through media experiences that enhance your lesson plans.

1. Sacramental Affects

At the beginning of this chapter, special effects were described as crafted illusory prompts intended to provoke the imagination. Imagination is the awakening of our senses to another dimension beyond our physical reality. In the movies, this kind of sensory transport from the ordinary to the extraordinary is the affect of audio, visual, and digital effects. The question is whether religious experiences provide us with a similar affect. There is no better place to begin that inquiry than with the special effects of the sacraments.

The sacraments are signs of God's presence in our midst. Most of us are so firmly entrenched in daily routine that it takes a special occasion to make us mindful of how God permeates all stages of our life from birth to death. The Catholic Church marks these stages with the seven sacraments: baptism, confirmation, Eucharist, reconciliation, anointing of the sick, holy orders, and matrimony. Each one of these sacraments is celebrated by a ritual that takes us out of the small picture of our individual lives into the big picture of the spiritual dimension. In other words, the sacraments take the story of the human-divine connection to the big screen. And like the movies, they are also accompanied by multi-sensory effects called sacramental effects or signs (e.g., water in baptism, rings in marriage, laying on of hands at ordination, oils for anointing). The following activity is intended to make students aware of the affect of both media and sacramental effects.

a. Begin the activity with a brief discussion of special effects in the media followed by a visual presentation of special effects from a movie clip appropriate to the age group. Ask students to identify the special effects in the movie and then to describe how the effects made them feel. Did the special effects enhance the story? Would they have experienced the story the same way without the effects? What do they think is the purpose of special effects?
b. If the point has not been made by the students, talk about special effects as prompts for the imagination. Does imagination have a role in our spiritual lives? Are there special effects in our religious practices? Talk about any sacramentals associated with the sacrament you are currently discussing. What is the purpose of these sacramental effects? For instance, how do they help tell the story of baptism or Eucharist? What is their symbolism? How did these sacramentals make you feel when you received the Eucharist for the first time or received the sacrament of reconciliation or were confirmed?

2. Sacramental Clips

This is a good follow-up to the previous exercise. Use film or a TV program to identify sacramental effects and affects in the media. How is water used in a film to signify new life? How is a meal used to symbolize communion? How is prayer used to move the character out of the smallness of his problem into the more generous space of divine intervention? You can create a list of such questions with the many symbols in Bible stories and in our sacramental rites.

3. Online: Blogging Sacramental Moments

This is a great collaborative activity to do during Advent or Lent. Talk about the human story behind each of the sacraments (e.g., baptism and birth; Eucharist and community; reconciliation and forgiveness). Although the sacraments make us aware of these stories in a special way, we actually experience birth, community, and forgiveness in our daily lives. See more about this activity online.

14
Core Concept #4: Media Are Businesses Organized for Profit and Power

> Then they came to Jerusalem. And he entered the temple and began to drive out those who were selling and those who were buying in the temple, and he overturned the tables of the money changers and the seats of those who sold doves.
> —*Mark 11:15*

In the famous scene from the 1976 movie *Network*, fired anchorman Howard Beale, the self-proclaimed "mad prophet of the airwaves" goes on television to incite audience rage. Barely able to contain himself, he tells his viewers across the country to raise their windows and rail against the manipulation of greedy television networks. Open it and stick your head out, and yell: "I'M MAD AS HELL, AND I'M NOT GOING TO TAKE THIS ANYMORE!"

The movie, a raucous rant against the abusive power of networks to exploit viewers for profit, was an instant box-office hit. It struck a raw nerve just beginning to quiver with the realization that our own stories and experiences are regularly usurped by commercial media and sold back to us for someone else's power and profit. But, it was a banner year in television with top-notch shows like *Mary Tyler Moore* and *All in the Family* riveting American audiences. Sr. Liz Thoman and a host of other real prophets of the airwaves were touting a kinder, gentler version of Beale's message but with hardly the same box office response. We weren't ready to take back the power even if unconsciously we understood that we didn't have it anymore.

THE POWER BROKERS

It is an old adage that whoever tells the story has the power. There was a time when that power was considered sacred and storytellers were revered. In tales passed down through generations, these wise women and men protected and preserved tradition, interpreted customs and mores, and transmitted the values of the collective culture. They shaped the world view of their people.

All that has changed with the disappearance of the tribal hearth. Until recently, the modernized version of that hearth was the town square where the schoolhouse, the community church, the local theater, and various mom-and-pop businesses formed an intimate gathering place for the telling of our stories. In many parts of the western hemisphere, those sacrosanct institutions of education, culture, commerce, and community have been replaced by the mall, the Cineplex theater (usually in the mall), the television, the cell phone, the iPod, and the Internet.

Notice what else is missing? Or should I rephrase the question: Who is missing? Take a closer look at your students' lives—plugged in, texting away, glued to the screen. As they consume and create the stories of their generation, again we have to wonder where are the teacher, the preacher, the parents who have traditionally had the responsibility of telling the stories. Standing in their place, carefully obscured behind the messages that they create, are the corporations that have made it a business of shaping our lives.

> *Online Activity: Who Is My Hero / Heroine*
> *Grades 1–12*
>
> Objective: To gauge the effect and the authority of media on the lives of our youth by examining who they consider to be their heroes and heroines.

THE MEN BEHIND THE CURTAIN

Let me introduce you to the storytellers. They are the new masters of the universe.

There are not very many of them. In 1983, when the first edition of *The Media Monopoly* was published, author Ben Bagdikian stated that fifty corporations controlled most of the media in the United States. That number shocked lots of folks who were used to the idea that their local paper and television station were autonomous and good-willed community messengers. Years later with the publication of the fourth edition (1992), Bagdikian announced that media ownership had dwindled to twenty-three corporations. Furthermore, he presented a dire scenario predicting that in the near future, the remaining media corporations would fold into about six international media empires. In 2006, *Mother Jones* magazine proved him just short of clairvoyance by reporting that all media was now in the hands of eight transnational corporations:

- Disney (market value: $72.8 billion)
- AOL-Time Warner (market value: $90.7 billion)
- Viacom (market value: $53.9 billion)
- General Electric (owner of NBC, market value: $390.6 billion)
- News Corporation (market value: $56.7 billion)
- Yahoo! (market value: $40.1 billion)
- Microsoft (market value: $306.8 billion)
- Google (market value: $154.6 billion)

These companies (see http://www.mediaowners.com/index.html) are like giant octopuses with greedy tentacles holding scores of other media outlets including newspaper chains (that's your local paper), radio stations (your favorite morning drive show), and amusement parks (you can see why information and entertainment get so mixed up), to name just a few of their assets.

THE GREATEST STORY EVER SOLD: CREATING THE WANT

As it turns out, what is an asset for the media barons is a liability for us. They are not teachers, preachers, parents, prophets, poets, visionaries—generally the type of people who are interested in telling a story for the health, education, and welfare of their audience. They are businesspeople. They do not tell stories. They sell stories. Their clientele are advertisers who buy time and space in the digital universe of television and radio programs, websites, and cell phones in order to reach their customers. In the minds and wallets of the media mavens, we are not listeners or viewers. We are consumers. A good example of how this perception works is MTV. The sole purpose for the creation and continued existence of MTV is to bring the teen/young adult audience—worth hundreds of billions of dollars in expendable income—to the network's sponsors.

What is particularly insidious about the storysellers is that they determine what stories will be told for profit. In its own defense, Madison Avenue claims that it is simply feeding the voracious appetite of American consumers by creating an ad-driven culture of instant gratification. But advertisers don't satisfy our appetite for "more"; they create a culture of "not enough." Underestimated as background noise, advertisements seep into our unconsciousness chanting, "Want, want, want, buy, buy, buy." Ironically, advertising with its careful and deliberate use of idyllic images, sacred symbols, and even religious concepts taps into those places of deep yearning that have traditionally been the holy ground of spiritual impulses. The objective, however, of the storysellers who run the media corporations is not to stir the soul, open the heart, engage the mind, or spark the imagination of the public but to make money. It's a business.

This may sound like a harsh indictment of the media industry, but it is not media bashing. It is media busting—a reality check on the balance of power between media makers and media consumers. Gospel work is always a reality check on the balance of power. Jesus was only twelve when he first entered the temple, the place where the stories of his religious tradition were told, and announced that he was about his Father's business. Years later, that business turned out to be challenging the moneychangers hawking their wares in the temple. Several days before he died, he again entered the temple in Jerusalem this time to confront the abuse of power and privilege. In an unmistakable expression of his anger, he "began to drive out those who were selling and those who were buying" (Mark 11:15). Long before the character of Howard Beale was dreamed up to portray a "mad prophet" in *Network*, Jesus took on that role in admonishing those who would tread upon sacred ground for power and profit.

> *Online Activity: The Media Moneychangers*
> *Grades 6–12*
>
> Objective: To make students aware of the intimate but complex web of corporate powers that own the media and sell our stories for profit.

THE GREATEST STORY EVER TOLD: RESPONDING TO THE NEED

The media minister, as custodian of the gospel story, must also check the balance of power. This means getting beyond the blame game of media makers versus media consumers to the core of the conflict. The profit margin of the media business demands that "wants" are created so that the public will then have "needs." These needs are then satisfied by products and services promoted by advertisers in order to subsidize media productions. How does the catechist respond to that world view?

The answer remains the same. We tell our story. We invert the Madison Avenue formula of "wants creating needs" with the gospel spirituality of "needs creating wants."

For years, advertisers and media barons have colluded to sell us what they think we want so that we will need it—buy it! And for millennia, the followers of the Gospel have been responding to spiritual needs of people through messages of forgiveness and healing. The hope is that we will want it and then live it! Unlike the media industry, which often reflects back to us pictures of reality that exclude groups of people who do not fit the profile of a good consumer (see Tool Box activity below), the Gospel offers a counterculture message of inclusivity. Unlike many media messages that court our primal instincts for competition and individual survival, gospel messages respond to primal longings for cooperation and community. One story says, "This is what you want." The other story asks, "What is it you need?" Which story are you going to tell? And even, more important, how are you going to tell it?

THE SOLUTION

Before you answer that last question, remember that audience manipulation for profit is a function of the economics of the media industry; it is not a characteristic of mass media in general. Therefore, it should come as no surprise that the most effective way to counter the abuse of media is to use the media. After all, Gospel is about witness—the silent language of prophecy. By bringing media stories of connection rather than consumption into your curriculum you are posing viable alternatives to commercialized values messages. Whether on television, in the movies, or on the Internet, there is no shortage of good storytelling. My experience has been that when you offer media fare outside of the usual blockbuster action films, students are mesmerized by the unexpected. In astonishment, they ask, "Where do you get these movies?" Seize that moment of surprise—the parable moment. It is the energy of transformation. That's our business!

THE TOOL BOX: MEDIA AND MORALITY AND SOCIAL JUSTICE

Spike Lee got it right in his movie *Do the Right Thing*. That simple statement pretty much sums up what it means to be a moral, righteous person. Morality gets complicated only because human beings are complex. We need morality spelled out because it is often hard to do the right thing, especially when it goes against our own self-interest. Catechesis teaches that the right thing means being loving, respectful, forgiving, virtuous, truthful, custodians of creation, just and kind participants in community, and in all things open to the wisdom of the Spirit in making choices. When we follow this path, it will lead us to serve the world. This is what the church calls social justice.

1. Media and Morality: What's In and What's Out

Looking at the above list of what constitutes moral behavior, how many of those attributes are the focus of media stories? Actually, many movies, TV programs, and documentaries tell wonderful stories of men and women making difficult moral decisions. The task for your students is to find those stories and discuss the moral lesson learned. It is also important to identify the stories that exploit immoral behavior. This is an exercise on "what's in" and "what's out" in terms of moral guidance in the media.

a. Begin by giving or showing examples of media that you think tell stories of exemplary moral conduct and those that do not.

b. Now turn the activity over to your students working in groups. Assign each group a specific moral virtue (see list above). Have them come up with one movie, TV program, or website where that virtue is "in." Next, find media where that virtue is "out." For example: What kinds of human behavior are typically covered in the evening news? What are not covered? Does war make the headlines more often than peace?

c. Which story did they prefer in their own groups? Why? Would one story be more profitable in terms of audience appeal than the other? Why? Who determines what audiences will like? How is the type of story effected by the profit margin? What stories are being told because they can be sold? Whose interests are involved? What types of stories are not told because they won't draw in the largest possible audience? Are there alternative media outlets for the untold stories? (For older students, this would be a valuable research assignment. Ask students in groups to find smaller, alternative media companies and present examples of their product to the class.)

d. Use this exercise to compare the moral authority of the media with the moral authority of the Gospel.

2. Who's In and Who's Out

Most importantly, stories are about people. According to media corporations, some people "sell" better than others. For example, how many television programs have people with disabilities as the main characters? What is the media trying to sell by picturing certain types of people and not others? These are the types of questions that will be addressed in this exercise.

a. Begin by giving or showing examples of media that tell stories of a diverse range of people followed by media that endorse a more exclusive picture of humankind.
b. Now turn the activity over to your students working in groups. Ask your students to replicate your presentation bringing in examples of media that are inclusive and exclusive in terms of the characters in the story. Think in terms of gender, race, ethnicity, religion, economic class, education, and different lifestyles.
c. Why are some people included while others are left out of the picture? Why are some people stereotyped? Is the way media picture our world, tell our stories, and image human beings fundamentally a social justice issue? Why would the profit margin be a motivator to leave some people out of the stories? Who makes that determination? Think of the talk shows and celebrity shows. Who's in? Who's out? Who cares? Does it matter?

15
Core Concept #5: Media Shape Values

Every year in April, the Center for SCREEN-TIME Awareness (CSTA) reminds Americans that it is time to turn off the television. For parents, teachers, and media advocates, "Turn Off Your TV Week" is a welcome rite of spring. The days are getting longer, the weather is getting warmer, time to get the kids off the video games, away from the television, unplugged from the iPod, and outside into a life.

The CSTA initiative is not a bad idea. They have disturbing facts to back up their claim that American children are turning into couch dumplings—overweight, overstimulated, and underachievers.[1] But here's the reality: As admirable as it might seem to suggest creative, quality family time as an alternative to television, we live in a mass media culture. We can turn the TV off for a week—and that's a good respite from the persistent onslaught of media messages—but we cannot turn the culture off even for a day. It is everywhere we are. It shapes us, molds us, and mirrors us. It is through the media culture that we continue to tell our stories. To disconnect from this culture would be like turning off the light on seeing ourselves.

A much more viable and durable option is to shed light on the situation by recasting the responsibility for creating responsible media. It is easy to point a finger at the media industry for their sins of commission. However, what about our sins of omission? Perhaps, we are part of the problem in our unwillingness to take seriously the media, the audience, the culture, the new ways we are learning, the new ways we must start teaching, the changing nature of our faith. Perhaps, we can be part of the solution by learning critical viewing skills and creating media worth watching.

THE WAY TO THE WAY

Where the problem ends, the solution begins. You are now at the end of this journey but the beginning of your adventure into the new territory of twenty-first-century catechesis. You have walked the way of the media pilgrim in order to lead the way as a media minister. Now it is time to show the way by taking on another mantle—that of the enlightened media maker who shapes responsible values through responsible media. Actually, all roads lead to here. The media maker is the pilgrim and the minister in action (Step 4 in the Empowerment Spiral on page 42).

The media maker is, of course, the ancient and still present storyteller who is entrusted with the task of forming and transforming human lives. As we have discussed in this book, some commercial media makers have exchanged that responsibility for power and profit (as have many storytellers throughout time). That sad fact of human history does not, however, excuse others from the very important prophetic work of reclaiming the stories. In the twenty-first century, this is a twofold process that involves (1) determining how media shape our values and (2) shaping values through media.

Much of this book has been a discussion of how media values shape our lives. Activities at the end of each chapter have provided you with lessons to integrate that exploration into your curriculum. The focus of this chapter, however, is to prepare you for the role of media maker through the creation of media that support catechesis.

Aha!

There's the parable moment—opening the doorway into the unexpected. Then there's the epiphany moment—the "aha!"—when you know that you have landed on the other side. This is exactly what happens when students (and adults) create media. Students learn that media is a construction of reality by constructing media. They learn that they have the power to create media, to be active agents of expression and change in their culture. They are no longer just the audience. They are the storytellers.

The Tool Box: Media Makers

Your students are already producing and distributing media in a variety of forms: creating Facebook pages, text messaging photos, burning CDs, creating short videos with their cameras or cell phones. But do they really know what they are doing? Do they understand the power, privilege, and responsibility of digital media communication?

1. Make Media!
Grades 6–12

Objective: To encourage your students to become responsible media makers by mentoring them through the process of creating media that reflect their worldview and values. This project requires the traditional cognitive skills of reading, writing, and researching in addition to production and critical thinking and critical viewing skills.

More than anything that you can say in the classroom, this exercise will provide your students with the awareness and the tools to become tomorrow's innovative and enlightened media makers.

Please go to the activities link for a detailed lesson plan on producing short films and documentaries.

2. Catechist Activity: Media Age Reflection Revisited

At the end of Chapter 3, you were asked to reflect on your understanding of the media culture from the perspective of a media pilgrim at the start of the journey. Now, as a seasoned pilgrim who has navigated the multifaceted terrain of the mediascape and as a media minister who is guiding your students into faith-informed participation in the media culture, we would like to know how you would describe the Age of Mass Media. A selection of responses will be posted on the link on the Paulist Press website. You are encouraged to do this exercise with your students. Review the descriptions of the Age of the Spoken Word and the Age of the Written and Printed Word in Chapter 3 to make a comparison. You might also want to consider some of these questions in your response:

1. When did the Age of Mass Media begin?
2. Who are the storytellers of this Age?
3. What story do they tell of humankind?
4. How have mass media changed the way we communicate with one another?
5. How has the media culture changed our perception of human possibility?
6. Has the Age of Media changed our perception of God? If so, how?
7. If the Age of the Spoken Word was the Age of God and the Age of the Printed Word was the Age of Humankind, who is at the center of the story in the Age of Mass Media?

THE NEW GENERATION OF MEDIA MAKERS

The person who tells the story has the power but that power does not come without responsibility. It is our task to teach that lesson. It is not enough to point out that media shape values. As mentioned in these pages many times, the Net Geners learn through the experience of doing and creating. By producing media in a variety of forms, students learn the subtleties of values transmission and information dissemination inherent in mass media constructions. They learn who and what is in and out of the picture. They learn how images tell stories with sounds and symbols that speak to our souls. They learn how audiences can be manipulated—and how often they are. They learn that creating media is not just entertainment but also a craft, a work of art, a journey into Divine Imagination.

Most importantly, as informed media producers, our children and youth today have the potential to become a new generation of media makers. They will learn to speak the language of their culture. They will learn to navigate their world with awareness and integrity. Holding onto the thread of Gospel and tradition, they will weave a new perspective of spirituality into the fabric of their culture. As the new threads are woven there will be a slow unraveling of the bindings of exploitation and manipulation to allow for the gradual emergence of leadership and vision in a media age. Such will be the legacy of the wisdom of the media pilgrim and the work of the media minister. Bravo!

Notes

Chapter 1

1. For the purposes of this book, "media culture" refers to twenty-first-century popular culture dominated and defined by electronic visual and digital mass media. Examples of electronic visual media include television and film. Examples of electronic digital media include the Internet, Twitter, iPods, cell phones, video games, CDs, e-books, and a growing array of interactive media.

Chapter 3

1. Ernest Kurtz and Katherine Ketcham, *The Spirituality of Imperfection: Storytelling and the Journey to Wholeness* (New York: Bantam Books, 1994), 7–8.
   This is a very old story that travels across many cultures. Depending on the time and place of the storyteller, the main character is a man or a woman, a rabbi, a priest, a midwife, a healer. This particular story is from the Jewish tradition. The ability of the story to adapt to different cultures attests to the universal appeal of its underlying truth.
2. *Catechism of the Catholic Church* (Liguori, MO: Liguori Publications, 1994), 13.
3. Karen Armstrong, *A Short History of Myth* (New York: Canongate, 2005), 13.
   "Everywhen" is a concept of timelessness particular to the spirituality of the Australian aborigines.

Chapter 4

1. Pierre Babin, *The New Era in Religious Communication* (Minneapolis, MN: Fortress Press, 1991), 152.

Chapter 6

1. According to the search engine Cuil (pronounced "cool"), there are more than 124 billion web sites on the Internet.

Chapter 7

1. Babin, *Religious Communication*, 146.

Chapter 8

1. John Pungente, SJ, and Monty Williams, SJ, *Finding God in the Dark: Taking the Spiritual Exercises of St. Ignatius to the Movies* (Boston: Pauline Books & Media, 2004), 13.
2. Rose Pacatte, FSP, "Catechetics and Media Literacy: Is There a Link?" *Word of Life* (September 1996).

Chapter 10

1. For more information on the Vatican's position on faith in an age of media and technology, see *Communio et Progessio* (Pastoral Instructions on Social Communications, 1971) and *Aetatis Novae*, published in 1992 as a twentieth-year anniversary homage to *Communio et Progressio*. Furthermore, the USCCB addressed the American Church directly in 1994 when it issued a statement making media awareness and education a pastoral priority.
2. Elizabeth Thoman and Tessa Jolls, *Literacy for the 21st Century* (Los Angeles: Center for Media Literacy, 2008), 8.
3. Ibid., p. 9.

4. Ibid., p. 42.
5. *Aetatis Novae*, 1992. Pontifical Council for Social Communication.

Chapter 11

1. Marc Prensky, "Engage or Enrage Me: What Today's Learners Demand," *EDUCAUSE* (September/October 2005): www.educause.net.

Chapter 12

1. Mike Hayes, *Googling God: The Religious Landscape of People in their 20s and 30s* (Mahwah, NJ: Paulist Press, 2007), 140.
2. Check out the *Frontline* website for this documentary and many others that explore the American cultural, political, and spiritual landscape: http://www.pbs.org/wgbh/pages/frontline/view/.
3. You can listen to the interview in its entirety at the homepage for the *Charlie Rose Show*: http://www.charlierose.com/guest/all/.
4. Karl Rahner, *Encounter with Silence*, trans. James M. Demske, SJ (South Bend, IN: St. Augustine's Press, 1999), 6.

Chapter 13

1. Babin, *Religious Communication*, 63.

Chapter 15

1. Check out "Facts and Information" on the CSTA website at: http://www.tvturnoff.org/.

OTHER BOOKS IN THIS SERIES

Connecting with Parents
Mary Twomey Spollen

Teaching the Faith
Kim Duty

Praying with Young People
Maureen Gallagher

Planning Your Teaching Year
Monica A. Hughes

How to Teach Scripture
Biagio Mazza